MW01233242

The Twelve Steps

:

A Spiritual Kindergarten

The Twelve Steps

A Spiritual Kindergarten

**Christian Perspectives
on the Twelve Steps**

Dale And Juanita Ryan

©1999 Dale and Juanita Ryan

Published by
Christian Recovery International
P.O. Box 215
Brea, CA 92822
714-529-6227
www.christianrecovery.com

All rights reserved. No part of this book may be reproduced or transmitted in any form or by any means, electronic or mechanical, including photocopying, recording, or any information storage and retrieval system, without written permission from the publisher, except for brief quotations in reviews.

Library of Congress Cataloging-in-Publication Data
The Twelve Steps: A Spiritual Kindergarten / Dale and Juanita Ryan
p. cm.
ISBN 0-941405-23-0 (pbk.)
1. Adult children of narcotic addicts—Religious life. 2. Adult child abuse victims—Religious life. 3. Adult children of dysfunctional families—Religious life. 4. Twelve-step programs—Religious aspects—Christians. I. Dale Ryan. II. Juanita Ryan III. Title: The Twelve Steps: A Spiritual Kindergarten

Scripture quotations, unless otherwise indicated, are taken from *The Holy Bible: New International Version*. Copyright © 1973, 1978, 1984 by International Bible Society. Used by permission of Zondervan Bible Publishers. All rights reserved.

The Twelve Steps are reprinted with permission of Alcoholics Anonymous World Services, Inc. Permission to reprint and adapt the Twelve Steps does not mean that A.A. has reviewed or approved the contents of this publication, nor that A.A. agrees with the views expressed herein. A.A. is a program of recovery from alcoholism only: use of the Twelve Steps in connection with programs and activities that are patterned after A.A., but that address other problems, does not imply otherwise.

Printed in the United States of America

The Twelve Steps

A Spiritual Kindergarten

Christian Perspectives on the Twelve Steps

Dale And Juanita Ryan

©1999 Dale and Juanita Ryan

Published by
Christian Recovery International
P.O. Box 215
Brea, CA 92822
714-529-6227
www.christianrecovery.com

All rights reserved. No part of this book may be reproduced or transmitted in any form or by any means, electronic or mechanical, including photocopying, recording, or any information storage and retrieval system, without written permission from the publisher, except for brief quotations in reviews.

Library of Congress Cataloging-in-Publication Data
The Twelve Steps: A Spiritual Kindergarten / Dale and Juanita Ryan
p. cm.
ISBN 0-941405-23-0 (pbk.)
1. Adult children of narcotic addicts—Religious life. 2. Adult child abuse victims—Religious life. 3. Adult children of dysfunctional families—Religious life. 4. Twelve-step programs—Religious aspects—Christians. I. Dale Ryan. II. Juanita Ryan III. Title: The Twelve Steps: A Spiritual Kindergarten

Scripture quotations, unless otherwise indicated, are taken from *The Holy Bible: New International Version.* Copyright © 1973, 1978, 1984 by International Bible Society. Used by permission of Zondervan Bible Publishers. All rights reserved.

The Twelve Steps are reprinted with permission of Alcoholics Anonymous World Services, Inc. Permission to reprint and adapt the Twelve Steps does not mean that A.A. has reviewed or approved the contents of this publication, nor that A.A. agrees with the views expressed herein. A.A. is a program of recovery from alcoholism only: use of the Twelve Steps in connection with programs and activities that are patterned after A.A., but that address other problems, does not imply otherwise.

Printed in the United States of America

Dedication

In memory of Luke Wainwright

Isaiah 61:1–3

Contents

Introduction

Welcome to Spiritual Kindergarten! It was Bill W., one of the founders of Alcoholics Anonymous, who first referred to the Twelve Steps as a "spiritual kindergarten." He was emphasizing that the Twelve Steps were designed to help us learn—and put into practice—the most basic spiritual truths. Spiritual Kindergarten is about the fundamentals of the spiritual life. It is first lessons. First steps. It is a back-to-basics, entry-level introduction to spiritual disciplines that unfortunately can be easily forgotten when we move on to more "advanced" concerns.

We know what it is like to forget the basics. It happens easily enough. It is all too easy to get excited about some new idea or trend and then find that we have lost touch with the most basic of things. But Christian spirituality has always placed a high value on the basics. Thomas Merton, in his book *Contemplative Prayer*, summarizes this well:

> One cannot begin to face the real difficulties of the life of prayer and meditation unless one is first perfectly content to be a beginner and really experience himself as one who knows little or nothing, and has a desperate need to learn the bare rudiments....We do not want to be beginners. But let us be convinced of the fact that we will never be anything else but beginners, all our life!

Jesus made the same point when he talked about the importance of being like children: "Let the little children come to me, and do not hinder them, for the kingdom of God belongs to such as these" (Mark 10:14). Jesus consistently honored and respected the simplest and most basic expressions of trust.

It is in this spirit that we invite you to enroll in Spiritual Kindergarten. Because it is for beginners, you don't have to worry about whether or not you are good enough, or smart enough, or ready enough to enroll. Whether you are an old-timer with the Twelve Steps or you have never seen them before—whether you have been a Christian for years or you are just starting to search for a meaningful spirituality—we believe that Spiritual Kindergarten can be helpful to you.

The Twelve Steps are best known, of course, as a collection of spiritual disciplines that have been helpful to people recovering from addictions. Whether the addiction is to alcohol, drugs, work, food, sex, "fixing" other people, or to anything else, the Twelve Steps offer the building blocks for a saner, freer, more grace-full way of life. If you struggle with one or more of these addictions, the Twelve Steps offer the hope of freedom from addiction's destructive trap.

You do not, however, need to be an addict to benefit from the Twelve Steps. The simple spiritual wisdom of the Twelve Steps can be helpful even if you do not struggle with an obvious addiction. We are all caught in fears, in defenses, and in patterns of behavior that are hurtful to ourselves and to others. These things often play a role in our lives that are very much like addictions. For example, we do the same things over and over again, expecting different results. We often find that we do things that we really don't want to do—even things we have promised not to do. The Apostle Paul, one of the leaders of the early Christian community, talked about this dynamic when he said: "I do not understand what I do. For what I want to do I do not do, but what I hate I do" (Romans 7:15). Whether you have an obvious addiction or, like the Apostle Paul, you struggle with the gap between your intentions and your actual behavior, the Twelve Steps offer the building blocks for a life-changing spiritual awakening.

As you anticipate using this book and working the Twelve Steps, it may be helpful to think about the Steps in four stages.

Stage one: peace with God. The first three Steps are focused on laying the foundation for peace in our relationship with God. We begin with the recognition that something has gone very wrong in our lives. Things are not as they should be. We need God's help. In this stage of the journey we admit our need for God, acknowledge God's power to help us, and make the decision to turn our lives over to his care.

Stage two: peace with ourselves. The next four of the Twelve Steps focus on laying the foundation for peace with ourselves. We inventory our lives. We take responsibility for our behavior. We come to the end of blame, avoidance, minimizing, and other self-protective strategies. We learn and put into practice new levels of honesty.

Stage three: peace with others. In Steps Eight, Nine, and Ten we turn our attention to doing the things that will make it possible for us to experience greater peace in our relationships with other people. Here we learn to practice the spiritual discipline of making amends for the harm we have done and find in this process the foundation for peaceful relationships.

Stage four: keeping the peace. Finally, in the last two Steps, we focus on actions that will allow us to maintain the peace that we have begun to experience as a result of our work in the earlier stages. We learn to practice the honesty, humility, love, and trust that we have been cultivating every day, in all that we do.

Each of the twelve chapters of this book explores one of the Steps. Each chapter begins with an examination of the Christian roots of the Step. This is followed by a study of a biblical text that relates to the Step. And finally, guidelines are provided for starting to put each Step into action.

We are convinced that the Bible can be a significant resource for understanding and working the Twelve Steps. We know that if you have experienced any form of spiritual abuse or have had the Bible used against you, you may find it difficult to imagine that the Bible could be helpful reading in Spiritual Kindergarten. However, the Twelve Steps have deep roots in Scripture. We encourage you to approach these texts with an open heart. It is our prayer that you will experience in these texts a surprisingly grace-full God.

It is important to emphasize that there is nothing magical about the Twelve Steps. They do not lead to a quick transformation that makes everything better. The Twelve Steps are not even a *cure* for alcoholism—or for anything else. *The Big Book of Alcoholics Anonymous* makes a much more modest claim for the Twelve Steps: "We are not cured of alcoholism. What we really have is a daily reprieve contingent on the maintenance of our spiritual condition." The Steps are tools for maintaining a healthy spiritual condition. Collectively they represent a path—a style of life—that can make it possible for us to receive from God the healing, the wisdom, and the grace we seek.

It is also important to know that the Twelve Steps are not the Twelve Concepts. They are not the Twelve Ideas or the Twelve Truths. They are twelve steps to take, twelve disciplines to practice, twelve activities to do. The focus is on action, not on ideas. You do the steps. If you merely believe the ideas that are found in the Twelve Steps, you cannot expect the desired results. As you work on each of the Twelve Steps in this workbook, we encourage you to focus on action. Ask yourself, *How can I do this today?* We have included a section at the end of each chapter to help you start finding ways to do that Step.

We want to encourage you, if at all possible, to use this book as a member of a group. It is the action orientation of the Twelve Steps that makes group participation so helpful. Step One begins with the word "we" for a reason. We can learn about the Steps by ourselves. But the strength and staying power needed for real change is much easier to acquire when we have group support. We encourage you to do whatever you need to do to find a community of people who can share the experience of Spiritual Kindergarten with you.

Our prayer is that you will find in Spiritual Kindergarten a grace-full path to travel and that, along the way, you will grow deep and satisfying relationships—with God, with yourself, and with others.

May you come to know yourself to be God's dearly loved child.

May your roots sink deeply into the rich soil of God's love.

Step 1

**Admitting
Powerlessness
and
Unmanageability**

*"If you always do what you always did,
you'll always get what you always got."*

About Step One

Who cares to admit complete defeat? Practically no one, of course. Every natural instinct cries out against the idea of personal powerlessness. It is truly awful to admit that, glass in hand, we have warped our minds into such an obsession for destructive drinking that only an act of Providence can remove it from us. But upon entering A.A. we soon take quite another view of this absolute humiliation. We perceive that only through utter defeat are we able to take our first steps toward liberation and strength. Our admissions of personal powerlessness finally turn out to be firm bedrock upon which happy and purposeful lives may be built.
—Anonymous, *Twelve Steps and Twelve Traditions*

People in the Twelve-Step programs know that until you're hurting enough, the Steps won't work for you. But for the fortunate sufferer, there comes a time when he or she says, "I've got to get well. I can't stand living like this anymore." And that is when one is ready for the miracles of the Twelve Steps.
—J. Keith Miller, *A Hunger for Healing*

Step 1

Admitting Powerlessness
and Unmanageability

Students in most classrooms begin with easy lessons and gradually progress to more difficult ones. In the Twelve Steps we begin with what some people experience as the most difficult lesson of all: no matter how powerful we may think we are, we are not powerful enough on our own to do what we want and need to do. On the surface it may seem like a simple lesson. There is nothing particularly complicated about it. Experience suggests, however, that it can be a very difficult lesson to learn. Alcoholics Anonymous makes this point simply in Step One:

> *We admitted we were powerless over alcohol—*
> *that our lives had become unmanageable.*

It is not easy to admit powerlessness. All of us want to maintain the illusion that we can manage our lives on our own. Eventually, however, we must all face the fact that there is a gap between our intentions and our ability to carry them out. This gap shows up in different ways for each of us. We may intend to stop drinking, but find that we are unable to do so for more than short periods of time. We may want to stop turning to food every time we feel sad or anxious, but find ourselves eating far beyond what we intended. We may want to be more expressive of our deepest feelings, but find ourselves emotionally withdrawn. We may promise ourselves that we will spend more time with our children, but continue to allow work to take priority. All of these gaps between our intentions and our actions are evidence of powerlessness.

We attempt to bridge the gap between our intentions and our behavior by trying harder to do things differently. But trying harder doesn't always work. In fact, sometimes the harder we try, the more unmanageable our lives become. Twelve Step programs begin with the admission that we cannot make the changes we need to make by using willpower alone. Whether we believe we are addicted or not, the lie that we are smart enough or competent enough or powerful enough to manage our lives on our own will eventually be shown for what it is—an attempt to play God. It takes courage to face our powerlessness. But the admission of powerlessness makes possible a dramatic spiritual change in our lives.

Step One: A Closer Look

We

The first word of Step One implies that healing takes place in community—not in isolation. This is not a new idea.

> *Two are better than one, because they have a good return for their work: If one falls down, his friend can help him up. But pity the man who falls and has no one to help him up! (Ecclesiastes 4:9, 10)*

The need for community is a major theme in biblical spirituality. God calls us to community—to close relationships with others. All of us are part of a family— God's family. That is why Jesus taught us to pray, "*Our* Father...."

Admitted

Spiritual kindergarten begins with the admission that we are in trouble. When we acknowledge this, we are ready to begin our spiritual journey toward peace and serenity. Admitting the truth is not something we can do casually. For most of us it represents a major change in business-as-usual. We have learned pretense, evasion, and denial. Now we must learn to admit the truth. The Bible puts a high value on telling the truth: "Each of you must put off falsehood and speak truthfully to his neighbor" (Ephesians 4:25). The falsehood that we "put off" in Step One is the belief that we do not need any help—that we can handle it, that we are managing our lives successfully on our own. In Step One we admit that this is not true. To our surprise, when we admit this truth, new and better ways of living become possible for us.

We Were Powerless

Being powerless does not mean that we are incompetent or helpless—or that we have no power at all. It means that we cannot rely on our will alone to achieve wholeness and peace. Willpower alone is not powerful enough. We see our powerlessness when we try to solve a problem through willpower (by determination, commitment, and trying harder) but find that the changes we achieve are only temporary. We may try to control the drinking or drug use of someone we love, but trying, trying harder, and trying our hardest will not make us powerful enough to achieve our objective. Or we may promise not to say yes to additional responsibilities, only to find ourselves taking on more and more obligations. If you have made promises, decisions, or choices and then found that your determination and commitment were not powerful enough to achieve the desired results, then you know what it is to experience powerlessness.

The Apostle Paul talked about powerlessness when he said, "I have the desire to do what is good, but I cannot carry it out" (Romans 7:18). Paul realized that the solution to his problem would need to involve more than just increased willpower. The central point of powerlessness is that willpower alone is not sufficient to enable us to make permanent changes. Trying harder didn't work for the Apostle Paul, and it doesn't work for us either.

Over Alcohol

The word "alcohol" in Step One can be replaced with other substances, behaviors, or conditions. Narcotics Anonymous, for example, replaces "alcohol" with "addictive substances." Some codependency groups replace it with "other people's choices." Some Christians use the word "sin" or "the effects of sin." The use of other words to replace "alcohol" allows anyone to use the Twelve Steps. The basic principles of the Steps are the same no matter what substance or behavior may be the focus of our addictive process.

Our Lives Had Become Unmanageable

What does it mean that our lives are unmanageable? It means that our efforts to manage our lives are not successful. Things are not working out according to our plan. We keep doing the things we think will solve our problems, only to find that our solutions are often worse than our problems ever were. There is an old slogan in A.A. that summarizes this: "I never had a problem that was worse than the old solution I found for it." Our lives become unmanageable because our "solutions" make things worse. We may eat because we don't want to feel so depressed, but the reality is that compulsive eating makes us *more* depressed. We may act out sexually because we don't want to feel so lonely, only to find ourselves more alienated than ever. We may run up large debts by buying new clothes so that we will feel less shame, only to feel the added shame that our spending is out of control. Solutions like these do not satisfy us for extended periods of time. The problems always return in one form or another. The prophet Isaiah was on target when he asked, "Why spend money on what is not bread, and your labor on what does not satisfy?" (Isaiah 55:2). Step One invites us to face the fact that our efforts to manage our lives have not worked. We will not be able to find better solutions until we have seen with clarity that our current solutions are part of the problem.

Step One Bible Study

Personal Preparation

1. What problem behaviors in your life motivated you to begin this study of the Twelve Steps?

_____

_____

_____

_____

_____

_____

_____

2. What difficulties do these problem behaviors create for you and for others?

_____

_____

_____

_____

_____

_____

_____

Biblical Text

There are many biblical texts that help to clarify Step One. In the text for this study, the Apostle Paul, one of the leaders of the early Christian community, talks about his own experience with powerlessness.

We know that the law is spiritual; but I am unspiritual, sold as a slave to sin. I do not understand what I do. For what I want to do I do not do, but what I hate I do. And if I do what I do not want to do, I agree that the law is good. As it is, it is no longer I myself who do it, but it is sin living in me. I know that nothing good lives in me, that is, in my sinful nature. For I have the desire to do what is good, but I cannot carry it out. For what I do is not the good I want to do; no, the evil I do not want to do—this I keep on doing. Now if I do what I do not want to do, it is no longer I who do it, but it is sin living in me that does it.

So I find this law at work: When I want to do good, evil is right there with me. For in my inner being I delight in God's law; but I see another law at work in the members of my body, waging war against the law of my mind and making me a prisoner of the law of sin at work within my members. What a wretched man I am! Who will rescue me from this body of death? (Romans 7:14-24)

Biblical Reflection

1. Paul describes his powerlessness as a tug-of-war. He wants "to do what is good," but he "cannot carry it out." What good things have you wanted to do—even promised to do—but found yourself unable to do with any consistency?

_____

_____

_____

_____

_____

_____

2. Paul says that doing good is not a simple decision. He continues to do what he does not want to do. There is a breakdown between his will and his behavior. He says, "The evil I do not want to do—this I keep on doing." What do you wish you could stop doing to yourself and to others?

_____

_____

_____

_____

_____

_____

3. We want to believe that we can control our lives and manage our affairs without help. In light of your answers to questions 1 and 2, what would you say is the truth about your ability to control and manage your life on your own?

_____

_____

_____

_____

_____

_____

4. To admit that our lives are unmanageable may seem like a defeat. But in fact, this admission reflects a willingness to be open to a new and healthier life. What feelings of defeat or failure do you experience when you think about how unmanageable your life has become?

_____

_____

_____

_____

_____

_____

5. In this text Paul talks about an internal warfare. It is the warfare between the part of us that wants to change and the part that resists change. How have you experienced this inner conflict?

_____

_____

_____

_____

_____

6. Paul describes himself as a prisoner of his own behavior and calls out for someone to rescue him. Describe a time when you felt like this.

_____

_____

_____

_____

_____

7. In a time of quiet, complete the following exercise:

Picture some of the behaviors that make your life unmanageable.
Experience the fear and sadness these behaviors cause.
Acknowledge your sense of being a prisoner of your own behavior.

Describe your experience of this time of reflection.

_____

_____

_____

_____

_____

_____

▶ Step One in Action

1. Admit aloud or in writing that you are powerless to make the changes you want to make on your own and that your attempts to do so are making your life unmanageable. Pay attention to the feelings you experience as a result of this admission.

2. In your daily affairs be aware of situations over which you are powerless. Keep a record of these situations.

3. In your daily affairs pay attention to behaviors and events that cause your life to be unmanageable. Keep a record of these things.

▼

We admitted we were powerless over alcohol— that our lives had become unmanageable.

▲

4. Put Step One into action by saying to yourself, "I am powerless over
_____, and pretending that I do have power is making my life unmanage-
able because _____." For example:

> "I am powerless over <u>my spouse's choices,</u> and pretending that I do have
> power is making my life unmanageable because <u>my effort to control my
> spouse's choices makes everybody angry</u>."

> Or

> "I am powerless over <u>my spending,</u> and pretending that I do have power is
> making my life unmanageable because <u>I am sinking deeper and deeper into
> debt.</u>"

▶ Step One Prayer

Dear God,
I don't seem to be able to manage my life.
I want to change.
But I can't seem to do it.
The things I think will help do not help.
Trying harder has not helped.
Blaming others has not helped.
Acting out has not helped.
Trying to control myself or others has not helped.
I am tired of this.
I can't do it.
I don't know what else to say.
Amen.

Step 2

Coming to Believe

*"If God is your copilot,
switch seats."*

About Step Two

When I came to Step Two I realized that although I was a committed
Christian and I really believed in God, my problem was that in some
very important respects I was living a frantic, highly stressed existence
as a Christian professional speaker and writer. I knew that something
was not right: I was teaching about grace and freedom, on the one hand,
and my life was anxious, stressful and over committed, on the other. But
I was in denial and couldn't see how bizarre the contradiction was.
People in this program have helped me to realize that anything I do or
think that is destructive to me or to my relationships with other people or
with God is a kind of insanity, especially when
I keep doing it month after month.
—J. Keith Miller, *A Hunger for Healing*

Few indeed are the practicing alcoholics who have any idea how irratio-
nal they are, or seeing their irrationality, can bear to face it. Some will
be willing to term themselves "problem drinkers," but cannot endure the
suggestion that they are in fact mentally ill. They are abetted in this
blindness by a world which does not understand the difference between
sane drinking and alcoholism. "Sanity" is defined as "soundness of
mind." Yet no alcoholic, soberly analyzing his destructive behavior,
whether the destruction of the dining-room furniture or his own moral
fiber, can claim "soundness of mind" for himself.
–Anonymous, *Twelve Steps and Twelve Traditions*

Step 2

Coming to Believe

In Step One we started to face the truth about the limitations of our own power. We recognized that our attempts to rely solely on ourselves caused our lives to be unmanageable. The next question is obvious: if *we* are not powerful enough to do what needs to be done, what hope is there? Where can we go to get the resources we need to live saner lives? Step Two of the Twelve Steps suggests that the solution to our problems is in a Power greater than ourselves:

Came to believe that a Power greater than
ourselves could restore us to sanity.

Some things are easy to believe. It is easy for most of us to believe that God will punish us. It is easy for us to believe that God will be displeased with us or that God dislikes us. What is difficult for many of us to believe is that God is more powerful than we are and that God is ready and able to use his power to help us. For a variety of reasons, many of us have distorted beliefs about God. We may fear that God is not very powerful—that God is weak or passive or disinterested in our lives. Or we may believe that God is powerful, but we fear that God will use his power to hurt us or to punish us. These distortions make it difficult for us to accept God's power—or God's willingness—to restore us to sanity. In Step Two we start the process of learning that God's power is *for* us, not *against* us.

▶ Step Two: A Closer Look

Came to believe

To believe means to put faith and trust in something or someone. In Step One we started to face the truth about our lives. In Step Two we come to believe in something or someone greater than ourselves. It is important to remember that God honors and responds to the smallest step of faith—even if it is mixed with uncertainty and disbelief. It is not necessary in Step Two to have absolute certainty and total confidence. Jesus said that faith as small as a mustard seed can move mountains (Matthew 17:20)! We may not have a lot of faith or trust when we enter spiritual kindergarten, but God can do a lot with what we have. Jesus emphasized this truth when he responded with compassion to a person who came to him for help saying, "I do believe; help me overcome my unbelief!" (Mark 9:24).

A Power Greater Than Ourselves

Step Two introduces a foundational spiritual truth: There is a God, and it is not me! In Step One we saw the results of our efforts to manage our lives on our own power. Now we can begin to look outside ourselves for the help we need. Remember Jesus' story about the prodigal son? (See Luke 15:11–32.) The prodigal son came to believe that he needed a Power greater than his own, so he decided to return home to his father. He expected his father to disown him and treat him like a slave. He did not know much about his father; he certainly did not understand his father's love and compassion. But the son did have enough faith to begin the journey home. Faith like that of the prodigal son is all we need in Step Two. At this stage of the journey we don't need sophisticated theology or years of Bible training. All we need is enough faith to get us headed toward a Power greater than ourselves. Later in the journey, we will learn much more about the Power who is helping us to make this change.

Could Restore Us

Notice that Step Two invites us to believe that restoration *could* happen. Step Two does not require us to believe that we *will* be restored. We may not yet be able to imagine that. We only need to believe that it *could* happen—if a Power greater than our own is available. That is why Step Two is sometimes called the "hope" Step. It introduces the possibility of restoration to sanity through a Power greater than ourselves.

Hope is a major theme of the Bible. Time after time throughout biblical history God's people have found themselves in difficult situations and have needed to find hope again in God's power. The psalmist lived through a number of these impossible situations and speaks about God's power to restore:

> *The LORD is my shepherd, I shall not be in want.*
> *He makes me lie down in green pastures,*
> *he leads me beside quiet waters,*
> *he restores my soul. (Psalm 23:1-3)*

In Psalm 107, the psalmist provides another dramatic image of God restoring his people to freedom:

> *They cried to the LORD in their trouble, and he saved them from their distress. He brought them out of darkness and the deepest gloom and broke away their chains. Let them give thanks to the LORD for his unfailing love and his wonderful deeds for men, for he breaks down gates of bronze and cuts through bars of iron. (Psalm 107:13–16)*

To Sanity

In Twelve Step programs, *insanity* is often defined as "doing the same thing over and over, while expecting a different result." For example, some of us use mood-altering substances (alcohol, drugs, nicotine, prescription medications, and so on) or controlling behaviors (manipulation, threats, avoidance, and so on) as our standard solution to life's problems. But the outcome is always predictable: we get more of the same chaos. Insanity in this context can be applied to any of us—even if we are not struggling with an addiction. We all tend to repeat the same kinds of self-defeating behaviors over and over again, expecting different results. The core of Step Two is coming to believe that there is a Power that could help us find a different, saner way to live. Things can improve, we can be healed, and our lives can become more peaceful and rewarding.

▶ # Step Two Bible Study

Personal Preparation

1. How does your life fit the definition of insanity—"doing the same thing over and over while expecting different results"?

_____

_____

_____

_____

_____

2. Describe any experiences you have had of being helped or restored by God's power:

_____

_____

_____

_____

_____

_____

Biblical Text

The text for this study is a psalm in which the author expresses his need for a Power greater than his own.

> *Hear, O LORD, and answer me, for I am poor and needy. Guard my life, for I am devoted to you. You are my God; save your servant who trusts in you. Have mercy on me, O Lord, for I call to you all day long. Bring joy to your servant, for to you, O Lord, I lift up my soul.*
>
> *You are forgiving and good, O Lord, abounding in love to all who call to you. Hear my prayer, O LORD; listen to my cry for mercy. In the day of my trouble I will call to you, for you will answer me.*
>
> *I will praise you, O Lord my God, with all my heart; I will glorify your name forever. For great is your love toward me; you have delivered me from the depths of the grave.*
>
> *The arrogant are attacking me, O God; a band of ruthless men seeks my life—men without regard for you. But you, O Lord, are a compassionate and gracious God, slow to anger, abounding in love and faithfulness. Turn to me and have mercy on me; grant your strength to your servant and save the son of your maidservant. Give me a sign of your goodness, that my enemies may see it and be put to shame, for you, O LORD, have helped me and comforted me.*
> *(Psalm 86:1–7, 12–17)*

Biblical Reflection

1. The author of this psalm is confident that God will help him. List the requests he makes of God in this text.

_____

_____

_____

_____

_____

_____

_____

2. People often fear that God will use his power to punish them. The psalmist is aware of his failures, yet he is confident that God is *for* him, not *against* him. List the words and phrases the psalmist uses to describe God.

_____

_____

_____

_____

3. How does this list compare or contrast with your image of God?

_____

_____

_____

_____

_____

4. People sometimes believe that they do not deserve God's help. The Bible teaches us that God is willing to help anyone who calls on him. What makes it difficult for you to believe that you can call on God for help?

_____

_____

_____

_____

_____

5. The psalmist wrote, "You are forgiving and good, O Lord, abounding in love to all who call to you." In what way could trusting this truth help you to call out to God?

_____

_____

_____

_____

_____

_____

6. Think of one or two situations in which you asked God for help. What did you ask for? What was the result?

_____

_____

_____

_____

_____

_____

7. The psalmist asks God for specific help. What specific help do you want to ask God to provide at this time?

_____

_____

_____

_____

_____

_____

_____

▶ Step Two in Action

You can put Step Two into action by paying attention to evidence that a Power greater than your own is at work. Make a list or a mental note of this evidence. Start with the most obvious and basic evidence—the things that we often overlook or take for granted. For example: "The sun came up this morning, and I was not in charge of that." Take some time every day to acknowledge other signs that there is a Power greater than your own. Include changes you see that you normally can't achieve, no matter how hard you try. For example:

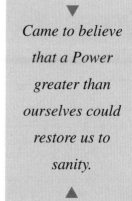

Came to believe that a Power greater than ourselves could restore us to sanity.

> "Today I was able to let go of trying to control my spouse, and let her handle the matter without telling her what to do and how to do it. The result

was a positive experience for both of us."

"Today I felt sad and lonely, but I didn't drown my feelings in food or alcohol."

Acknowledge these evidences of a Power greater than your own by reciting a prayer or by making notes in a journal. A simple prayer like "Thank you, God" is sufficient. A note that reads "I received the help I needed today" is a gentle reminder that a Power greater than your own is at work.

▶ **Step Two Prayer**

Dear God,
I pray for an open mind and heart
so that I may come to believe
more fully, more deeply in you—
in your power and in your love.
I pray for humility
and for an opportunity
to increase my faith in you.
Amen.

Step 3

Deciding to
Trust God

"Let Go and Let God"

About Step Three

Like all the remaining Steps, Step Three calls for affirmative action, for it is only by action that we can cut away the self-will which has always blocked the entry of God—or, if you like, a Higher Power—into our lives. Faith, to be sure, is necessary, but faith alone can avail nothing. We can have faith, yet keep God out of our lives. Therefore our problem now becomes just how and by what specific means shall we be able to let Him in? Step Three represents our first attempt to do this. In fact, the effectiveness of the whole A.A. program will rest upon how well and earnestly we have tried to come to "a decision to turn our will and our lives over to the care of God as we understood Him."
–Anonymous, *Twelve Steps and Twelve Traditions*

Billy Graham tells a story that beautifully illustrates how faith necessarily entails trust, which is needed as we move beyond the belief of Step Two into the commitment of Step Three. To paraphrase the story: A brave man pushes a wheelbarrow back and forth along a tightrope suspended high above Niagara Falls. The crowd watches in astonishment as the agile acrobat continues to push the wheelbarrow back and forth over the deadly, roaring falls. Then the man places a 200-pound sack of dirt in the wheelbarrow and boldly makes his way across the falls, pushing the heavy load through the misty air. Making his way back, the tightrope walker points to a man in the crowd and asks, "Do you believe I can push a man in the wheelbarrow across the falls?" The excited onlooker says, "Yes, of course." The acrobat points directly at the man and says, "Get in!" Step Three is about getting into the wheelbarrow.
–Martin M. Davis, *The Gospel and the Twelve Steps*

Step 3

Deciding to Trust God

The Twelve Steps begin with an admission that we cannot manage life on our own. In Step Two we added to this foundation a belief that God could do for us what we cannot do for ourselves. These first two Steps have prepared us to make an important decision. The first three Steps have often been summarized in three simple statements: "I can't. God can. I think I'll let him." Step Three encourages us to make a decision to turn our lives over to God's care:

> *Made a decision to turn our will and our lives over to the*
> *care of God as we understood Him.*

Most of us know intellectually that God can care for us a lot better than we can care for ourselves. But we may be afraid to trust God to care for us. We may have trusted other people who turned out to be untrustworthy. As a result, we might not expect any caregiver—even God—to be kind or helpful. Even though we may know that God is grace-full and loving, we may experience fear when we start to make the decision suggested by Step Three.

Making a decision is all that is required of us in Step Three. It is similar to planning a vacation. First we decide to go on a vacation, then we start making plans for the vacation, and then we actually take the vacation. The decision is a very important part of the process—but it is not the *whole* process. In Step Three we are only making a decision. We don't need to trust God completely and totally for the rest of our lives in order to do Step Three. We start by making a decision to turn our wills and lives over to God's care *today*. It is a decision we will need to make one day at a time for the rest of our lives. Each day that we choose to entrust our lives to God's care, our trust in God's wisdom and love will grow.

► Step Three: A Closer Look

Made a Decision

This Step invites us to make a decision. The decision we make is to turn our life and our will over to God's care. This decision will begin a lifelong process of change that can lead to peace and serenity. We do not need to understand the entire process in order to begin. It is enough to know that we cannot do it on our own. The actual process of "turning it over" will come later. It is clear in Scripture that God is aware of the choices we face and that he wants us to make good choices:

> *I have set before you life and death, blessings and curses. Now choose life, so that you and your children may live and that you may love the LORD your God, listen to his voice, and hold fast to him. (Deuteronomy 30:19, 20)*

To Turn

The word *surrender* is often used to describe the "turn" of Step Three. It is a decision to give up on our own will and to surrender our will to a Higher Power. The word *surrender* can be a confusing word, because it sounds like a sign of weakness or failure—of "giving up" or "losing." Many people who start working on Step Three are afraid that if they turn their lives over to God, they will have no life left—that they will lose everything. But just the opposite is true. What has led to all of the losses in our lives is our refusal to surrender control to God. What will lead to serenity and peace is our willingness to surrender to God. Jesus captured the heart of Step Three when he said:

> *"Whoever finds his life will lose it, and whoever loses his life for my sake will find it." (Matthew 10:39)*

We have worked very hard to "find" our lives—to control our lives and to be in charge of everything we do. But the result has been loss. Jesus says that if we "lose our lives"—if we surrender our lives and turn over our lives to God—then we will find our lives for the first time.

Our Will and Our Lives

What is it that we decide to turn over to God? Our broken wills. And our broken lives. That is what we decide to give to God in Step Three—broken wills and broken lives. It might not seem like much of a gift. But that is because we do not yet understand all that God can do with broken stuff. Nor do we yet understand how different God's good and gracious will is from our own wills. In Step Three we choose to turn our broken wills and our broken lives over to God. We do so in the hope that God will do a better job with our lives than we have done. There will be many pleasant surprises ahead on the journey as we begin to see the results of this decision. The psalmist expressed the hope that comes from surrender to God:
> *Teach me to do your will, for you are my God;*
> *may your good Spirit lead me on level ground. (Psalm 143:10)*

Over to the Care of God

In Step Three we entrust our lives to God's care. What will it be like for God to care for us? At this stage of the journey some of us may have terrible and frightening images of what this will be like. It may feel like turning ourselves over to a judge who will punish us severely—or even like turning ourselves over to an executioner. But that is not what it is like to be cared for by God. God is a good caregiver. Things have gotten worse and worse as long as we have been in charge of our own care. With God in charge of caring for us, things will get better. Jesus often emphasized the kindness of God's loving care. For example, Jesus talked about how we exhaust ourselves trying to carry our own burdens. We are invited, Jesus says, to a very different kind of life, in which we turn our burdens over to God:

> *"Come to me, all you who are weary and burdened, and I will give you rest." (Matthew 11:28)*

As We Understood Him

Some people—Christians in particular—may not see a need for this part of Step Three. Some have changed these words to read "through Jesus Christ." It is understandable that those of us who are Christians would want to make that change. But it is also important to remember how useful it is to keep the door of spiritual kindergarten open for everyone. You do not need to have a complete understanding about God—or about Jesus—to benefit from this Step. We are still in spiritual kindergarten. We won't get very far if we must pass an examination in theology before we make use of the Twelve Steps.

The phrase "as we understood Him" does *not* suggest that we already know everything we need to know about God. Our understanding of God will change as we work through the Twelve Steps. The phrase "as we understood Him" means only that we act on the basis of what we have learned in Step Two—that God's power is greater than our own and that God is powerful enough to restore us. That's all the faith we need when we work on Step Three. It may seem to some people that this is just a little bit of faith. But as Jesus taught, God can do great things with a little bit of faith.

> *"I tell you the truth, if you have faith as small as a mustard seed, you can say to this mountain, 'Move from here to there' and it will move. Nothing will be impossible for you." (Matthew 17:20)*

Step Three Bible Study

Personal Preparation

1. What fears do you have about turning your will and your life over to God's care?

_____

_____

_____

_____

_____

_____

2. What problems in your life motivate you to want to turn your life over to God's care?

_____

_____

_____

_____

_____

_____

Biblical Text

The text for this study is part of a psalm in which the author invites us to turn our lives over to God. It then talks about the loving care we can expect to receive from God.

> *Trust in the LORD and do good; dwell in the land and enjoy safe pasture.*
> *Delight yourself in the LORD and he will give you the desires of your heart.*
> *Commit your way to the LORD; trust in him and he will do this:*
> *He will make your righteousness shine like the dawn, the justice of your cause like the noonday sun. (Psalm 37:3-5)*

Biblical Reflection

1. This psalm invites us to turn our lives and our wills over to God's care. The psalmist uses specific words to describe what to do when we entrust ourselves to God. The first word he uses is "trust." To trust is to rely with confidence on someone or something. How would you describe your current level of confidence or trust in God?

_____

_____

_____

_____

_____

_____

_____

2. The second word the psalmist uses is "delight." To delight is to find joy or pleasure in someone or something. What experiences have you had of finding joy or pleasure in God?

_____

_____

_____

_____

_____

3. The third word the psalmist uses is "commit." To commit is to give or to entrust something to someone for safekeeping. In what ways are you beginning to commit yourself to God and to his loving care?

_____

_____

_____

_____

_____

4. What does the psalmist say will be the benefits of entrusting our lives to God?

_____

_____

_____

_____

_____

5. What benefits do you hope to receive as you turn your life over to God's care?

_____

_____

_____

_____

_____

6. Picture God as someone you can rely on with confidence—as someone in whom you can find joy and pleasure. Think of him as someone to whom you can entrust your life for safekeeping. What thoughts and feelings do you have as you think of God in this way?

_____

_____

_____

_____

_____

7. Write a short prayer expressing whatever trust you have in God, whatever delight you feel toward God, and whatever desire you have to commit your life to God today.

_____

_____

_____

_____

_____

Step Three in Action

1. Write a short letter to God, telling him that you have decided to turn your life over to his care. Include any concerns you have about how this is going to work and any hopes you have about what the results will be.

2. Each day pray the Lord's Prayer, with special focus on the phrase "Your kingdom come, your will be done."

3. As part of your daily activities, practice saying "I give this to you, God" when a difficult situation arises or when you are not sure what to do. Stay open to God's guidance and provision. Thank God for any signs of his caring presence.

▼

Made a decision to turn our will and our lives over to the care of God as we understood Him.

▲

Step Three Prayer

Lord, I am learning that there are lots of things I can't do.
I can't control life.
I can't make people be what I want them to be.
But there is one thing I can do.
I can make a decision to turn my will and my life over to you.
Making this decision doesn't mean I know how to make it happen.
Making this decision doesn't mean I understand you or your plan.
Making this decision doesn't even mean I'm entirely willing.
But it does mean that I believe you can do a better job
of managing my life than I have done.
I am ready to entrust my will and my life to you, God.
Make something better of it than I have.
I can't. You can. I've decided to let you.
Amen.

Step 4

Taking
Inventory

*"Having a resentment is like drinking poison
and expecting someone else to die."*

About Step Four

Imagine you are transferring the ownership of your life to God in the same way you would transfer ownership of a business. One of the first things you would do in negotiating to sell a business would be to take an inventory to discover the damaged or out-of-date goods that are no longer salable. In Step Four we call it a "moral" inventory because we compile a list of traits and behaviors that have transgressed our highest, or moral, values. We also inventory our "good" traits and the behaviors that represent them. In our life's moral inventory the defects or dysfunctional behaviors might include some that once worked; some dysfunctional behaviors may have saved our lives as children, but they are now out-of-date, self-defeating, and cause us a great deal of trouble when we use them as adults.
—Keith Miller, *A Hunger for Healing*

Step Four is our vigorous and painstaking effort to discover what these liabilities in each of us have been, and are. We want to find exactly how, when and where our natural desires have warped us. We wish to look squarely at the unhappiness this has caused others and ourselves. By discovering what our emotional deformities are, we can move toward their correction. Without a willing and persistent effort to do this, there can be little sobriety or contentment for us.
—Anonymous, *Twelve Steps and Twelve Traditions*

► *Step 4* ◄

Taking Inventory

In the first three Steps we established the foundations for a closer relationship with God. We gave up trying to be God ourselves, we acknowledged God's power, and we made a decision to turn our wills and our lives over to God's care. In the next few Steps, we will build on this foundation as we begin to develop a new relationship with ourselves. We will deepen our self-awareness by looking with honesty and courage at ourselves and at our behaviors. In Twelve Step programs this discipline of self-awareness is called making an inventory:

Made a searching and fearless moral inventory of ourselves.

The process of looking closely at ourselves in Step Four will be challenging. It is like opening the door to a messy closet. Our first response may be to feel overwhelmed or depressed by the mess. Sorting and organizing everything in this closet may seem like an impossible task. As we start to sort through the mess we may have strong emotional reactions to some of the discoveries we make. We may become sad, depressed, or angry. We may feel deep shame and guilt. It will be important to remember that no matter what we find in the process, our problems do not make us unworthy or unloved by God. In the inventory process we will discover things that we did not know were there. Some of our discoveries will be treasures worth keeping, and others will be things that need to be discarded.

The inventory process will lead us to a more honest and realistic assessment of who we are. This deeper self-awareness will open the door to new possibilities, new choices, and new freedom in our lives.

► Step Four: A Closer Look

Made a Searching
"Searching" implies that we are looking for something that may be hidden or that may be difficult to identify. Therefore, we will need to be diligent and thorough in our search. For many of us, making an inventory will be a new experience. Many of us have worked hard to avoid this kind of disciplined self-searching. We will need to recognize our tendencies to avoid painful truths and to blame others for our problems. A wholehearted effort to look honestly at ourselves will be necessary if we are to be successful in Step Four.

Step Four does not suggest that we are responsible for everything that happens or that we are the sole source of all our problems. We may have been harmed in many ways. Although this is an important factor that we need to acknowledge, the purpose of Step Four is to identify the things for which *we* are responsible. We cannot fix anyone else or be responsible for the poor choices that other people make. What we are able to do is to take an honest look at our own behavior.

Working Step Four requires that we look honestly and compassionately at ourselves. Fortunately, God is prepared to help us do this. A good start might be to adopt as our own the prayer of the psalmist:

> *Search me, O God, and know my heart; test me and know my anxious thoughts. See if there is any offensive way in me, and lead me in the way everlasting. (Psalm 139:23, 24)*

Fearless

Calling this self-examination "fearless" doesn't mean that we won't be afraid. That's too much to expect of anyone. It's only natural to experience some fear. We will need to ask God to give us the courage that will make it possible for us to work on this Step in spite of our fears. When we are willing to proceed in spite of our fears, the reward will be worth the effort. It may help to remember that, although we will experience fear, it is not God's intention that fear control our lives. Fear is often connected with the expectation of punishment, and God's intentions are *not* to punish us but to help us become free of our fears as we grow in love:

> *There is no fear in love. But perfect love drives out fear, because fear has to do with punishment. (1 John 4:18)*

Moral Inventory of Ourselves

A moral inventory is not a new idea. The Old Testament assumes that it will be a part of the life of God's people: "Let us examine our ways and test them, and let us return to the LORD" (Lamentations 3:40). The early Christian church practiced this spiritual discipline in the context of community worship. The Apostle Paul said, "A man ought to examine himself before he eats of the bread and drinks of the cup" (1 Corinthians 11:28). The moral inventory we take in Step Four is not intended to cause shame. It is an opportunity to look at ourselves honestly and thereby prepare ourselves to make positive changes. Although there will be some discomfort in this process, the end result will be lives marked by greater freedom and grace.

Step Four Bible Study

Questions for Personal Preparation

1. Hesitation or procrastination are common reactions to the idea of doing a moral inventory. What fears or concerns might lie at the root of your hesitations?

_____

_____

_____

_____

_____

_____

2. What support or assistance would help you as you make your inventory?

_____

_____

_____

_____

_____

_____

Biblical Text

Learning to tell ourselves the truth is a major theme in the Bible. This text, from a letter written to the first Christian communities, talks about living a life characterized by truth.

> *This is the message we have heard from him and declare to you: God is light; in him there is no darkness at all. If we claim to have fellowship with him yet walk in the darkness, we lie and do not live by the truth....I am writing you a new command; its truth is seen in him and you, because the darkness is passing and the true light is already shining. Anyone who claims to be in the light but hates his brother is still in the darkness. Whoever loves his brother lives in the light, and there is nothing in him to make him stumble. (1 John 1:5, 6 and 2:8–10)*

Questions for Biblical Reflection

1. This text begins by stating: "God is light; in him there is no darkness at all."
What images come to your mind as you read these words?

_____

_____

_____

_____

_____

_____

_____

2. This text tell us that God's light is the light of love. How does this compare or
contrast with your images of God's light?

_____

_____

_____

_____

_____

_____

_____

3. How might it help you, as you anticipate making your inventory, to realize that
God's light is the light of *love*—and that inviting God to shine his light into
your life is to invite God's love into your life?

_____

_____

_____

_____

_____

_____

_____

4. As this text teaches, to the extent that we love others, we are living in God's love—living in God's light. To the extent that our relationships are not characterized by love, we are still in darkness. Think about two or three of your closest relationships. What signs are there that you are acting in loving ways in these relationships?

_____

_____

_____

_____

_____

_____

_____

5. What signs are there of a lack of love on your part in each of these relationships?

_____

_____

_____

_____

_____

_____

6. The text says, "the darkness is passing and the true light is already shining." The text does *not* say we are perfect. It says that a process of change and healing is taking place. What specifically would it look like for the darkness to pass and for the light to shine in your relationships?

_____

_____

_____

_____

_____

_____

_____

7. In a time of quiet, picture God and his loving light shining on you, surrounding you, and filling you. In love, God helps us see what needs to be corrected, what needs to be changed, what needs to be healed. Stay with this prayerful meditation for several minutes. Write whatever thoughts, feelings, and images came to you during this time.

_____

_____

_____

_____

_____

_____

▶ Step Four in Action

If this is the first time you have done a moral inventory, you will probably not be able to complete a comprehensive inventory. Do as much as you can in the time you have available. This process can be revisited at any time. There are many ways to do a moral inventory. Here are three suggestions that may help you to structure your inventory process:

1. Spend time focused on the image "God is light." Let the light of God's loving, healing presence shine into all the parts of your life. God's light is gentle but bright. There is no darkness when God's light is present. Let God's light reveal who you are: your strengths, your weaknesses, your sins, your fears, your gifts. As you continue with this awareness of God's light shining on you, write freely about your experience; do not edit your writing or worry about sentence structure or grammar. Write whatever thoughts and feelings come to you as a result of God's light. Write without stopping for ten to twenty minutes.

Made a searching and fearless moral inventory of ourselves.

2. Prepare a sheet of paper for each six-year segment of your life. Label each page with the appropriate time period (birth through age six, ages seven through twelve, and so on). On each page write whatever memories come to you (you may need more than one page for each time span). You may want to have four sections for

each time period: (1) memories—both positive and painful, (2) any actions on your part that were harmful to you or to someone else, (3) your positive actions and experiences, and (4) ways you can see that God took care of you. Be as specific with names, dates, events, and behaviors as you can.

3. Prepare a separate sheet of paper for parents, siblings, spouse, children, friends, coworkers, God, and self. On each page list any harm you have done in these relationships. Also list any positive and loving contributions you have made. Be sure to include a page about the harm you have done to yourself.

▶ ## Step Four Prayer

Dear God,
I have looked into the closet of my life.
It is a mess.
I have no idea how it can be sorted out.
Help me to identify the things that need to be discarded.
And help me to identify the things that deserve to be preserved.
Give me the courage, compassion, grace, and strength I need to do this task.
Amen.

Step 5

Admitting
Our Wrongs

*"If you share your pain you cut it in half,
if you don't you double it."*

About Step Five

The thing to do with sin is to do what Nicodemus did: go and
search out someone with whom we can talk privately and
frankly. Tell them of these things and, with them as witness,
give these sins and our old selves with them, to God. You say
that you can do this alone with God; and I ask you, Have you
succeeded in doing so? I said I was going to do that for years,
but it never happened until I let a human witness
come in on my decision.
—Samuel Shoemaker, *National Awakening*

All of A.A.'s Twelve Steps ask us to go contrary to our natural
desires...they all deflate our egos. When it comes to ego defla-
tion, few steps are harder to take than Five. But scarcely any
step is more necessary to longtime sobriety
and peace of mind than this one.
—Anonymous, *Twelve Steps and Twelve Traditions*

Step 5

Admitting Our Wrongs

In Step Four we made our inventory. As a result, we have a more realistic view of our lives. Now it is time to start doing something about it. So what do we do after we have taken a realistic look at our lives? Our inclinations may be to try to forget some of our painful discoveries. But that is the opposite of what Step Five suggests. In Step Five we admit our wrongs:

> *Admitted to God, to ourselves, and to another*
> *human being the exact nature of our wrongs.*

Admitting our wrongs is a form of confession. In Step Five, confession is a three-part process. First, we admit our wrongs to God. Then we admit them to ourselves. Lastly, we share our wrongs with another human being.

This process can be a powerful, life-changing experience. The spiritual discipline of admitting our wrongs is a process that can free us from the pain and remorse we feel about our past behavior. It is a difficult path, but it leads to the grace-full way of living that we all desire.

▶ Step Five: A Closer Look

Admitted

Both the Bible and Christian tradition emphasize the importance of confession—of admitting our wrongs. Unfortunately, there are many people who have minimal experience with confession. There are also many people whose experience with confession has been shaming and hurtful. Step Five provides an opportunity for us to practice this spiritual discipline in a way that is respectful and healing rather than shaming and hurtful.

To admit that we have done something wrong is not easy. Many of us have concealed the truth and have been afraid to admit our wrongs to ourselves or to anyone else. We are experts at blame, evasion, deception, and denial. It will be a challenge to reverse these patterns. But learning to admit our wrongdoing can lead us to a richer and more satisfying life.

To God

Many of us are reluctant to tell God the truth. We may want to pretend that God doesn't know about our faults. We may not want to confess our sins to God because we don't know how God could love someone who behaves as we do. We may think that silence is the best course of action. But there is no real freedom without confession. Silence about our wrongdoing only makes the pain worse. The psalmist describes the depression, insomnia, and stress that can come when we keep silent about our wrongs:

> When I kept silent,
> my bones wasted away
> through my groaning all day long.
> For day and night
> your hand was heavy upon me;
> my strength was sapped
> as in the heat of summer.
> Then I acknowledged my sin to you
> and did not cover up my iniquity.
> I said, "I will confess
> my transgressions to the LORD."
> (Psalm 32:3–5)

When we admit our wrongs to God, a great weight is lifted. Remember that there is nothing you can do or confess that would cause God to stop loving you. The Bible is clear and explicit about this; *nothing* can separate us from the love of God. If fear and shame get in the way during this part of Step Five, you might read Romans 8:38 several times to remind you of this fundamental truth.

> For I am convinced that neither death nor life, neither angels nor demons, neither the present nor the future, nor any powers, neither height nor depth, nor anything else in all creation, will be able to separate us from the love of God that is in Christ Jesus our Lord. (Romans 8:38)

Now try reading this verse aloud, as follows: "Nothing, including [*the first item in your inventory*], can separate [*your name*] from the love of God." Do this for each inventory item.

To Ourselves

We are the principal victims of our lack of honesty, and eventually we pay a high price for our self-deceit. We may try to convince ourselves that we can bury our wrongs and never have to admit them. But eventually we will have to face the fact that dishonesty does not work to our advantage. The Bible says it like this: "If we claim to be without sin, we deceive ourselves and the truth is not in us" (1 John 1:8).

In Step One we started to see the truth. We admitted our powerlessness and the unmanageability of our lives. In Step Four we made an inventory and accepted the truth about our past behaviors. In Step Five we take full ownership of our Step Four inventory and accept the painful realities we identified. This may take some time. It is painful to allow the truth about our wrongs to "sink in" to the point where we can say that we have "admitted" them.

An important element of this part of Step Five is to respond to our own admission of wrong. Many of us have learned to respond to our own failures, shortcomings, and wrongs with judgmentalism and shame. Now we have an opportunity to show mercy to ourselves. We can face our failures with compassion—the same compassion that God extended to us in the first part of Step Five. This is one reason why confession to God comes *before* confession to ourselves; we can learn something about how to respond to ourselves by experiencing God's grace-full, compassionate response to us.

To Another Human Being

It is possible to work through the first four Steps in isolation from other people. It is not a *good* idea, but it is possible. However, Step Five requires us to talk to another person. Scripture is clear about this: "Confess your sins to each other and pray for each other so that you may be healed" (James 5:16). The idea of sharing our faults with another person can be threatening, because we may anticipate experiencing guilt, shame, and rejection. Sharing with another person makes it real in a new way. When we confess to another person it prevents our inventory from becoming a private little secret between God and ourselves. Experience has shown that we can manage to hold on to much of our denial if our confession is only to God and to ourselves. Making a full confession to someone who understands, who is compassionate, and who shares experiences similar to our own helps keep us honest and on track.

The Exact Nature of Our Wrongs

One way that we protect ourselves from the full impact of Step Five is to fall back on generalities. That is why in Step Five we admit the "exact nature" of our wrongs. If we say, "I have a problem with time management," that is a general statement. It is more useful to say "I missed my son's soccer game last week because I lost track of time. I placed more importance on my work than I did on my promise to attend his game." The specifics are what connect us with the full emotional reality of what we have done—with the pain that our actions created for ourselves and for others. Acknowledging the specifics opens our hearts to what Scripture calls "godly sorrow," which is a form of grief that causes us to take seriously the impact of our actions:

> *Godly sorrow brings repentance that leads to salvation and leaves no regret, but worldly sorrow brings death. (2 Corinthians 7:10)*

▶ Step Five Bible Study

Questions for Personal Preparation

1. What fears do you have as you prepare to admit your wrongdoing to God, to yourself, and to another person?

_____

_____

_____

_____

_____

_____

_____

2. What benefits do you expect to receive from admitting your wrongs?

_____

_____

_____

_____

_____

_____

_____

Biblical Text

The text for this study is a prayer that expresses some of the inner struggle that accompanies the work of Step Five.

Have mercy on me, O God, according to your unfailing love;
according to your great compassion blot out my transgressions.
Wash away all my iniquity and cleanse me from my sin.
For I know my transgressions, and my sin is always before me.
(Psalm 51:1–3)

Questions for Biblical Reflection

1. In this text, the psalmist calls on a God whose love is unfailing and whose compassion is great. How does this description of God compare with your expectations of God?

   _____

   _____

   _____

2. How would it be easier for you to admit your wrongs to God if you anticipated that God would respond to you with love and compassion?

   _____

   _____

   _____

   _____

3. The psalmist says, "I know my transgressions, my sin is always before me." We have an increased awareness of our wrongs as a result of our Step Four inventory. In what way is your behavior different as a result of this increased awareness of your wrongs?

   _____

   _____

   _____

   _____

   _____

4. The psalmist asks for God's mercy. As we admit our wrongs to God, to ourselves, and to another human, it is important that we receive mercy. Mercy is a respectful, empathic, forgiving love. Think of a time when you have extended mercy to someone or a time when you received mercy from someone. Write about what you experienced.

_____

_____

_____

_____

_____

_____

5. Picture yourself admitting your wrongs to God. Picture God responding with mercy toward you. Write your response to this image.

_____

_____

_____

_____

_____

_____

_____

_____

6. Picture yourself admitting your wrongs to yourself. Picture yourself responding with mercy. Write your response to this image.

_____

_____

_____

_____

_____

_____

7. Picture yourself admitting your wrongs to another person. Picture that person responding with mercy. Write your response to this image.

_____

_____

_____

_____

_____

Step Five In Action

Step Five has three parts. We admit the exact nature of our wrongs first to God, then to ourselves, and finally to another person. Use the inventory you made in Step Four to remind yourself of the wrongs you need to confess.

1. Admitting our wrongs to God
Select a time to talk to God about the wrongs you have identified. You can do this part of Step Five in a number of ways. Whether you write, speak aloud, or pray quietly, the result will be the same. Don't be concerned if tears are part of this process; they are a natural reaction to the work we do in Step Five.

Admitted to God, to ourselves, and to another human being the exact nature of our wrongs.

2. Admitting our wrongs to ourselves
Schedule a specific time and place to do this part of Step Five. Read your Step Four inventory to yourself. The goal is to acknowledge and take full personal ownership of everything it includes. Some people find it helpful to write themselves a letter as a response to their confession. Find some practical way to extend kindness and mercy to yourself as part of this process.

3. Admitting our wrongs to another human being
It may take some time to select a person to hear your confession in Step Five. The person you select needs to understand the importance and limited goals of this Step. He or she must be able to observe strict confidentiality. You need to be able to trust that person. A close friend, a sponsor, a therapist, or a pastor are possible

choices. It is important to clarify your expectations of the other person; be clear about what you need. If you want feedback, say so and talk about the kind of feedback you want. If you want only to be heard, make sure the listener knows this. When you have finished, take time to acknowledge your accomplishment.

▶ Step Five Prayer

Dear God,
I want to confess the exact nature of my wrongs to you.
Help me to trust in your unfailing love.
Help me to trust in your great compassion.

I want to confess the exact nature of my wrongs to myself.
Help me to take full responsibility for the choices I have made.
Help me to be as compassionate with myself as you have been with me.

I want to confess the exact nature of my wrongs to another person.
Help me to find someone who can hear my confession with compassion.
Help me to find someone who can receive my story without condemnation.
Amen.

Step 6

Preparing
for Change

*"Our defects of character are the bars of a cage.
The central point is not to study the bars,
but to get out of the cage."*

About Step Six

[Step Six] is A.A.'s way of stating the best possible attitude one can take in order to make a beginning on this lifetime job. This does not mean that we expect all our character defects to be lifted out of us as the drive to drink was. A few of them may be, but with most of them we shall have to be content with patient improvement. The key words "entirely ready" underline the fact that we want to aim at the very best we know or can learn....Only Step One, where we made the 100 percent admission we were powerless over alcohol, can be practiced with absolute perfection. The remaining eleven steps state perfect ideals. They are goals toward which we look, and the measuring sticks by which we estimate our progress. Seen in this light, Step Six is still difficult, but not at all impossible. The only urgent thing is t
hat we make a beginning, and keep trying.
—Anonymous, *Twelve Steps and Twelve Traditions*

When we tried to clean ourselves up with our own power and "discipline" we kept ourselves agitated, confused, in denial, and worn out, and we were in almost constant emotional pain. We were like the man who tore the scab off his arm every morning to see if his wound had healed. But it was in doing the sixth step that I saw why I had become so exhausted. I'd been trying to do God's part in the spiritual growth and healing process. In the program I was told that my part was "being entirely ready," being ready to let God be the controller and life-changer of myself and others. When I did that, my sponsor said, I would see how God's power is released to flow through our lives to clean them only when we quit trying to control the how and when he is to use that power.
—Keith Miller, *A Hunger for Healing*

Step 6

Preparing for Change

In Step Four we made an inventory of our lives. In Step Five we admitted the truth about our lives to God, to ourselves, and to another person. Now the time has come to get ready for God to change us:

Were entirely ready to have God remove
all these defects of character.

Change is difficult. Even changes that we want to make are difficult. So we need to prepare ourselves for the change process. In Step Four we identified patterns of behavior that have been hurtful to us and to others. These negative patterns are defects of character that developed in our lives over a long period of time. Some examples of character defects are blaming others, controlling others, isolating ourselves, and numbing our feelings. We may have observed during our inventory that we use blame to protect ourselves from realities that we do not want to face. Or we may have observed that we withdraw from the people closest to us whenever there is a conflict. Or we may have seen how we medicate ourselves with chemicals, food, TV, or work to avoid feeling emotional pain. These and other behaviors are often survival skills that helped us at one time in our lives. But they are no longer helpful to us. They have turned into character defects—patterns of behavior that are hurtful to us and to others. In Step Six we prepare ourselves to let God change these well-established behavior patterns.

▶ Step Six: A Closer Look

Were Entirely Ready

After all the work we have done on the first five Steps, you might think that we would be ready—if not eager—for God to remove our defects of character. So why is a whole Step reserved for getting ready for this to happen? Unfortunately, the character defects that we identified in our inventory are often behavior patterns that we think are important for our survival. When we were children these behavior patterns may have protected us, given us some sense of control over our lives, or helped us to stay at a distance from intolerable circumstances. For example, silence and isolation may have helped us to feel safer in a frightening home

– 57 –

environment. But that same strategy, which once seemed so helpful and necessary, is now part of our problem. Part of becoming "entirely ready" for God to change us is to admit that we have become attached to these behaviors and that letting go of them may not be easy.

The process of becoming "entirely ready to have God remove all of our defects of character" is similar to grieving. We are losing something that once seemed valuable to us. Grieving will take time and may involve some sadness. But grieving is a necessary part of letting go. As we go through the grieving process, however, we will find comfort and peace. We will learn healthier, more productive, and more joyful ways to live! Jesus put it this way: "Blessed are those who mourn, for they will be comforted" (Matthew 5:4).

Notice that the goal in Step Six is not speed; we do not seek to get ready as fast as possible. The goal is thoroughness; we seek to become *entirely* ready. Step Six allows us the time necessary to grieve the loss of the defects we must give up. It is a time to prepare for God to do spiritual and psychological surgery on our character.

To Have God Remove

We get ready, but it is God who removes our character defects. We do the asking. God does the work. As we learned in Step One, we do not have the power to do what needs to be done. Our focus needs to be on becoming ready. If we think we can make the changes by ourselves, we will find ourselves trying harder and harder—and getting more and more frustrated by our inability to change. When it comes to change, our task is to "let go and let God," or as God says through the psalmist "Be still, and know that I am God" (Psalm 46:10).

All These Defects of Character

Having God remove *all* of our defects may sound like a huge task. It *is* a big task. But God's plans for us involve more than just a superficial makeover. The changes we are preparing for are fundamental ones. Changes in character go down to the core, to bedrock, to our foundation. God's intentions are to do a heart transplant: "I will remove from them their heart of stone and give them a heart of flesh" (Ezekiel 11:19).

This change process will require patience from us. We cannot expect everything to happen overnight. Deep and lasting changes in patterns established over many years will take time. God understands that we will not be "entirely ready" to have him remove "all" of our defects of character all at once.

Step Six Bible Study

Personal Preparation

1. What character defects identified in Step Four are the most frustrating for you?

_____

_____

_____

_____

_____

_____

_____

2. What problems do these character defects create in your life?

_____

_____

_____

_____

_____

_____

_____

Biblical Text

Defects of character are the patterns of behavior that we hoped would satisfy us but have instead harmed us and others. In this text the prophet Isaiah reminds us that God invites us to come to him—to allow him to heal us, to change us, and to give us a deeply satisfying life.

> "Come, all you who are thirsty, come to the waters; and you who have no money, come, buy and eat! Come, buy wine and milk without money and without cost. Why spend money on what is not bread, and your labor on what does not satisfy? Listen, listen to me, and eat what is good, and your soul will delight in the richest of fare....

> "Let the wicked forsake his way and the evil man his thoughts. Let him

turn to the LORD, and he will have mercy on him, and to our God, for he will freely pardon....

"You will go out in joy and be led forth in peace; the mountains and hills will burst into song before you, and all the trees of the field will clap their hands. Instead of the thornbush will grow the pine tree, and instead of briers the myrtle will grow. This will be for the LORD's renown, for an everlasting sign, which will not be destroyed."
(Isaiah 55:1, 2, 7, 12, 13)

Biblical Reflection

1. The first part of this text describes an unsatisfying lifestyle. In Step Four we identified many behaviors that were ultimately unsatisfying. Review your Step Four work. What have you spent time, money, and energy on that has left you unsatisfied?

_____

_____

_____

_____

_____

_____

_____

_____

2. In this text God invites us to receive, free of charge, food that will satisfy us and delight our souls. Write a short prayer responding to this invitation from God.

_____

_____

_____

_____

_____

3. In the second part of this text, God calls us to forsake our wicked ways and evil thoughts—our character defects. When we review our Step Four inventory we identify patterns of behavior that in Step Six are called "defects of character." What defects of character have you observed as a result of working the first five Steps?

_____

_____

_____

_____

_____

_____

4. Which of these character defects are you ready to have God remove?

_____

_____

_____

_____

5. What character defects are you hesitant to have God remove?

_____

_____

_____

_____

6. This text teaches us that the God who calls us to a more deeply satisfying life is also a God of mercy who will freely pardon us. How might this truth help you become ready for God to remove your defects of character?

_____

_____

_____

_____

_____

_____

7. The last section of this text is a promise of new life. It is a picture of the joy that we will receive as we allow God to heal and change us. As we become ready for God to remove our defects of character, we begin to see more clearly how our lives can be improved as a result of God's work. What good things do you anticipate will be made possible by your readiness to let go of your defects of character?

_____

_____

_____

_____

_____

_____

▶ Step Six in Action

Step Six is about getting ready to have God change us. Like Advent, the period just before Christmas, it is a season of preparation and anticipation. During Advent we prepare our hearts in anticipation of the coming of Christ.

Over the years many Christians have developed rituals that help them prepare their hearts for this season of the year. Perhaps some outward expression might also nurture an inward readiness when we work on Step Six. Consider a Step Six exercise for yourself. Can you think of any outward symbol that would help you to remember that the changes that God will bring to your life are good ones? Here are two possible suggestions.

▼

Were entirely ready to have God remove all these defects of character.

▲

One person began her Step Six ritual with a bag filled with birdseed. The bag of seed represented all the things that kept her from being "entirely ready." She took a walk each day with the bag of seed and her list of character defects. On each walk she reviewed her list. With each reading, she grew in her willingness to release her defects to God. She symbolized that release by tossing the birdseed into the air. After several walks and readings and releases, the bag was empty and her heart was ready.

Another idea is to write on a separate piece of paper each character defect you have identified. Put all the pieces of paper into a box labeled "What I want God to remove." Label another box "What I am ready to have removed." When you are ready for God to remove a particular defect, move that paper to the second box. Each time you move a paper to the "ready for removal" box say a short prayer thanking God for the readiness you have received.

These are just examples of the kinds of exercises that might be helpful. Does any exercise or ritual come to your mind? Write it out and put it into action.

_____

_____

_____

_____

_____

_____

_____

_____

▶ Step Six Prayer

Quiet my heart, God.
Help me to open my heart to your love.
Help me to open my heart to your good gifts.
I want to truly desire the changes you have prepared for me.
So quiet my heart.
Make me ready.
Amen.

Step 7

**Asking God
to Change Us**

*"Humility is not thinking less of yourself,
but thinking of yourself less."*

About Step Seven

The whole emphasis of Step Seven is on humility. It is really saying to us that we now ought to be willing to try humility in seeking the removal of our other shortcomings just as we did when we admitted that we were powerless over alcohol, and came to believe that a Power greater than ourselves could restore us to sanity. If that degree of humility could enable us to find the grace by which such a deadly obsession could be banished, then there must be hope of the same result respecting any other problem we could possibly have.
—Anonymous, *Twelve Steps and Twelve Traditions*

The biggest change the humility of Step Seven brings is in our relationship with God. He is no longer the "helper" who helps us get our agenda on track so we can accomplish what we want. He is the "owner of the business," and we are trainee employees, learning the business and our part in it one day at a time.
—J. Keith Miller, *A Hunger for Healing*

Step 7

Asking God to Change Us

The first three Steps allowed us to make peace in our relationship with God. We did this by admitting our need for help, by realizing the existence of a Power greater than ourselves, and by making a decision to give ourselves over to God's care. This is just a beginning. Hopefully, we will continue for a lifetime to grow in our relationship with God. Starting in Step Four, we shifted our focus to building a more peaceful relationship *with ourselves*. As part of this process, we made an inventory, admitted our wrongs, and became ready for God to remove our shortcomings. Step Seven brings us to the end of this second stage of the Twelve Step journey. We are ready now to ask God to remove our shortcomings. Step Seven shows us how to proceed when we are entirely ready for God to change us:

Humbly asked Him to remove our shortcomings.

In Step Seven we ask God to remove our shortcomings. We cannot, however, expect to have all of them removed immediately. Step Seven is not magic. We will not be immediately transformed into new people. It will take some time to do the asking. We will be able to make some requests promptly, but others will require more preparation on our part.

▶ Step Seven: A Closer Look

Humbly

Humility is the spiritual foundation of Step Seven. But what is humility? The prophet Isaiah provides a helpful image of the humility we seek in Step Seven. He said, "We are the clay, you are the potter" (Isaiah 64:8). The clay can become a useful pot only with the help of the potter. This is the biblical theme of God as Creator. We are God's creation. God is the potter. We are the clay. We deceive ourselves completely if we try to be the potter. Practicing humility teaches us to accept the role of the clay and to let go of attempts to be the potter. We are a lump of clay that can become a magnificent pot if we have the humility to let God take charge of our lives!

Humility is the opposite of grandiosity. But it is important to emphasize that humility has nothing to do with *humiliation*. It has nothing to do with thinking that we are bad or unworthy. There is no shame in humility. The humility we seek in Step Seven is based on an honest and accurate assessment of who we are. With humility we are able to stop trying to "look good." We can stop trying to manage how other people perceive us. With humility we are able to think and feel about ourselves more accurately—with less grandiosity and less shame. Humility contributes significantly to our serenity, because it frees us from so much of what causes us to feel anxious and burdened. Jesus summarizes it well when he says, "Whoever exalts himself will be humbled, and whoever humbles himself will be exalted" (Matthew 23:12).

Asked Him

The idea of asking for something may feel awkward to us. There are many reasons for this. As children, our requests may have fallen on "deaf" ears—so we learned not to ask. We may see no reason to ask God because he already knows what we want or need. After doing our fourth Step inventory, some of us feel a sense of shame at the thought of asking anything of God. But asking is a necessary part of the process of change. Jesus talks about the benefits of asking for help:

> Which of you, if his son asks for bread, will give him a stone? Or if he asks for a fish, will give him a snake? If you, then, though you are evil, know how to give good gifts to your children, how much more will your Father in heaven give good gifts to those who ask him! (Matthew 7:9–11)

To Remove Our Shortcomings

The Twelve Steps use a variety of words to describe the problems we face. Some of these words are *unmanageability*, *insanity*, *wrongs*, *defects of character*, and *shortcomings*. Each description emphasizes a slightly different aspect of the problems we have created for ourselves. The word "shortcomings" in Step Seven is similar to one of the words translated as "sin" in the Bible. It means "to miss the mark," as an archer might miss a target. We have definitely missed the target, as our work in Step Four made very clear. Now in Step Seven we ask God to change us so that we can be "on target" again.

What we ask for in Step Seven is the removal of our shortcomings. We don't ask for help in adapting to them or for help in managing them. We don't ask for help in continuing to live with them. We want them removed. And that's what we ask for.

We have spent many years developing the character defects that we are now asking God to remove. As a result, some of our requests for the removal of character defects may be granted promptly, but others may require patience and perseverance. When we become discouraged or frustrated with God's timing, we may be tempted to take back control of the process. But it may help us to sustain hope if we review the work we have done in earlier Steps. Seeing our progress may help us remember how much better off we are in God's care, even if change sometimes seems unbearably slow. The removal of our shortcomings is now in God's hands. A master craftsman of souls is at work. God can be trusted to do a good job, because he cares about his work—and he cares about us:

> *Humble yourselves, therefore, under God's mighty hand, that he may lift you up in due time. Cast all your anxiety on him because he cares for you." (1 Peter 5:6, 7)*

▶ Step Seven Bible Study

Questions for Personal Preparation

1. Imagine that your life is a garden and that your shortcomings are the weeds. Which shortcoming has caused you the most trouble? Describe a recent situation in which this behavior pattern has manifested itself as a problem or concern.

_____

_____

_____

_____

_____

_____

2. Which of the shortcomings you have identified are you most reluctant to give up?

_____

_____

_____

_____

_____

_____

Biblical Text

The text for this study is a prayer in which the psalmist asks God to remove his shortcomings.

Cleanse me with hyssop, and I will be clean; wash me, and I will be whiter than snow. Let me hear joy and gladness; let the bones you have crushed rejoice. Hide your face from my sins and blot out all my iniquity. Create in me a pure heart, O God, and renew a steadfast spirit within me. Do not cast me from your presence or take your Holy Spirit from me.

Restore to me the joy of your salvation and grant me a willing spirit, to sustain me. Then I will teach transgressors your ways, and sinners will turn back to you. Save me from bloodguilt, O God, the God who saves me, and my tongue will sing of your righteousness.

O Lord, open my lips, and my mouth will declare your praise. You do not delight in sacrifice, or I would bring it; you do not take pleasure in burnt offerings. The sacrifices of God are a broken spirit; a broken and contrite heart, O God, you will not despise.
(Psalm 51:7–17)

Questions for Biblical Reflection

1. In the Bible study for Step Five we looked at the first part of this psalm. The psalmist began by confessing his wrongdoings to God. Now the psalmist asks God to remove his shortcomings—to help him and to change him. List the specific requests that the psalmist makes.

   _____

   _____

   _____

2. Which of the psalmist's requests do you want to adopt as part of your own requests to God?

   _____

   _____

   _____

   _____

3. Write a brief psalm of your own asking for God's help.

_____

_____

_____

_____

_____

4. The psalmist asks God to restore his joy and to make major changes in his life. Write a short prayer asking God to restore joy to your life.

_____

_____

_____

_____

_____

5. What images come to mind when you picture God "restoring" joy to you?

_____

_____

_____

_____

_____

6. In the last part of this text the psalmist tells us that God values "a broken spirit" and "a broken and contrite heart." These phrases describe the spiritual humility we need in Step Seven. We *humbly* ask for God's help because we know that we cannot, by our own power, remove our defects of character. How has a lack of spiritual humility affected your life?

_____

_____

_____

_____

_____

7. What increase in humility do you see in your life as a result of practicing the Twelve Steps?

_____

_____

_____

_____

▶ Step Seven in Action

1. Use your inventory from Step Four to make a list of your shortcomings. For each shortcoming, identify the new behavior you want to receive when God removes the shortcoming from your life. For example:

Humbly asked Him to remove our shortcomings

My shortcoming: I try to manipulate and control other people.
My desired new behavior: With God's help I will be able to let my coworkers do things their way.

My shortcoming: I isolate myself from people.
My desired new behavior: With God's help I will be more trusting and be able to reach out in appropriate ways to others.

2. Ask God to remove each of the shortcomings you identified.

3. List examples that show how God is already working to free you from your shortcomings.

4. Take time to thank God in prayer for the progress you have made at this point in the journey.

▶ Step Seven Prayer

Dear God,
I pray that you will remove every shortcoming
that stands in the way of my learning to love others
as you have loved me.
Amen.

Step 8

Willingness to
Make Amends

*"We're responsible for the effort,
not the outcome."*

About Step Eight

It had been embarrassing enough when in confidence we had
admitted these things to God, to ourselves, and to another human
being. But the prospect of actually visiting or even writing the
people concerned now overwhelmed us, especially when we
remembered in what poor favor we stood with most of them.
There were cases, too, where we had damaged others who were
still happily unaware of being hurt. Why, we cried, shouldn't
bygones be bygones? Why do we have to think of these people
at all? These were some of the ways in which fear conspired
with pride to hinder our making a list of
all the people we had harmed.
—Anonymous, *Twelve Steps and Twelve Traditions*

In Steps Eight and Nine we learn that the way out of the pain of
separation is through that pain, not around it. Instead of justify-
ing ourselves, we own our hurtful behavior specifically. Instead
of burying what we find, we go to the person we have offended,
confess the behavior, and make amends. For those of us who
have always hated to be wrong and have been terribly afraid of
rejection, this is a very frightening prospect. When I had been in
the program long enough to be at Step Eight I had heard many
people talk about the serenity and restored relationships that
came from doing Steps Eight and Nine, and I was at least ready
to do Step Eight. I was desperately afraid of Step Nine, but my
sponsor reminded me that I only had to do one step at a time;
I could wait until I was ready—even if it took years.
So I began Step Eight.
—J. Keith Miller, *A Hunger for Healing*

Step 8

Being Willing to Make Amends

The first seven Steps helped us to establish the beginnings of a more peaceful relationship with God (Steps One through Three) and with ourselves (Steps Four through Seven). In Step Eight we begin the process of establishing a more peaceful relationship with others.

Many of the strategies we have used to manage our relationships have been unhelpful. When we have had problems in our relationships, we have pretended that the problems didn't exist. Or we have avoided the people with whom we had conflicts. Or we have blamed others for all of the problems. Strategies like these have not led us to peaceful relationships. The Twelve Steps suggest that making amends is the most important thing that we can do to bring peace to our relationships. If we want to make peace, we need to set aside our tendencies to pretend, deny, avoid, blame, argue, forget, or evade. We need to replace these unhelpful strategies wherever possible with making amends. In Step Eight we begin the amends process by making a list of the people we have harmed and by becoming willing to make amends to them:

> *Made a list of all persons we had harmed,*
> *and became willing to make amends to them all.*

Making a list of people we have harmed can cause us to feel uncomfortable. We may experience feelings of fear, shame, and guilt when we start thinking about making amends. But there is no need to feel that doomsday is approaching. Making amends will, in some cases, lead us to restored relationships! The number of people who will greet our efforts to make amends with open arms may surprise us. Restored relationships will not always be the outcome. In all situations, however, there will be significant rewards for becoming willing to make amends. Making amends can make it possible for us to let go of some of the emotional burdens we have been carrying. We will gain the confidence that comes from knowing that we have taken full responsibility for our own behavior.

Step Eight: A Closer Look

Made a List

The first part of Step Eight is based on the work we did in Step Four. In Step Four we made a moral inventory of our lives. In Step Eight we revisit this inventory in order to make a list of the people we have harmed. As we start to make the list, our tendency may be to rationalize, minimize, or avoid some of our actions. We may think, *Let bygones be bygones*, or *That was a long time ago*, or *Don't make such a big deal out of it*. We may think that people have forgotten about what happened. Regardless of our resistance or rationalizations, we need to make the list anyway.

It is important to include *ourselves* on the list of people we have harmed. The harm we have done to ourselves because of our behavior has an impact on how we feel about ourselves today. As we get a clearer picture of the harm we have done to ourselves and become willing to make amends to ourselves, we will grow in compassion for ourselves and in our capacity to respect and value ourselves.

Of All Persons We Had Harmed

It is normal in Step Eight to think about the people who have harmed us and what they did to hurt us. The spiritual growth that Step Eight makes possible, however, will come only if we focus on the behaviors for which *we* are responsible. For our own spiritual benefit we must focus our attention on how we have harmed others— not on how they have harmed us. The only sins we need to focus on and make amends for are our own. We can't change what others have done to us, but we can become willing to make amends for what we have done to others.

A list of people we have harmed is *not* the same thing as a list of people who don't like us, or a list of people we would like to please. The goal of the first part of Step Eight is to make a list of the *people we have harmed*. The focus on *harm* in this Step is important. It is intended to protect us from making a list of "people we would like to see changed." Our focus needs to be on *our* actions that caused *harm* to others, not on how to get other people to like us or to feel good about us.

Became Willing to Make Amends

The second part of Step Eight is similar to Step Six, in that it involves a time of preparation. In Step Eight we don't actually make amends; we focus on the will-ingness to do so. What does it mean to be willing to make amends? We know that some people will respond to our amends with gratitude and support. In these cases, willingness to make amends may be relatively easy. In other situations, however, willingness can be quite difficult. For example, we need to be willing to make amends to people who have harmed us. When the harm done *to* us seems much larger than the harm done *by* us, willingness can be much more difficult.

Becoming willing to make amends will be easier if we work toward forgiveness for any harm done to us. Offering forgiveness to people who have harmed us is a good thing. The Bible puts a high value on forgiveness: "Be kind and compassionate to one another, forgiving each other, just as in Christ God forgave you" (Ephesians 4:32). But forgiveness is often a long and challenging journey. We do not need to be at the end of that journey before we become willing to make amends. We need to remember that the task of Step Eight is *not* to forgive others for the harm they have done to us; it is to become willing to make amends to others for the harm we have done to them. This is something we can do even if our forgiveness is still in process.

In addition to working on forgiveness, we can increase our willingness to make amends by preparing ourselves for the kinds of responses we may receive from others. Some people will welcome our amends. Other people, however, may reject us when we try to make amends. In such cases, willingness to make amends will be much easier if we prepare ourselves by gathering a supportive community of people around us who can encourage us when we experience rejection. Supportive friends and companions can encourage us to do whatever is necessary to make amends.

We need to make amends even if our forgiveness has not yet proceeded to completion and even if we expect to receive responses that will be difficult for us. It is not reasonable for us to expect that all of our amends will be easy. Sometimes we need the willingness to make amends to people who have profoundly mistreated us and who are not likely to respond in healthy ways to our amends. The Bible is, however, clear about such situations:

> *"Love your enemies, do good to those who hate you, bless those who curse you, pray for those who mistreat you." (Luke 6:27, 28)*

In difficult cases, becoming willing to make amends may require us to "do good to those who hate" or to "bless those who curse." We need, in such circumstances, to remind ourselves that we are not making amends to change someone else. We are not doing this *for* someone else. We are doing this for *ourselves*. We are making amends because we want to move on in life, to become saner people, and to find more serenity in life.

Step Eight Bible Study

Questions for Personal Preparation

1. How would you describe your current willingness to make a list of people you have harmed?

_____

_____

_____

_____

2. What fears are you aware of that might get in the way of your willingness to make amends?

_____

_____

_____

_____

3. What reactions do you have to including *yourself* on your amends list?

_____

_____

_____

_____

_____

Biblical Text
The text for this study is from the teaching of Jesus on our attitudes toward other people:

> *"Do not judge, and you will not be judged. Do not condemn, and you will not be condemned. Forgive, and you will be forgiven. Give, and it will be given to you. A good measure, pressed down, shaken together and running over, will be poured into your lap. For with the measure you use, it will be measured to you."*

He also told them this parable: "Can a blind man lead a blind man? Will they not both fall into a pit? A student is not above his teacher, but everyone who is fully trained will be like his teacher.

"Why do you look at the speck of sawdust in your brother's eye and pay no attention to the plank in your own eye? How can you say to your brother, `Brother, let me take the speck out of your eye,' when you yourself fail to see the plank in your own eye? You hypocrite, first take the plank out of your eye, and then you will see clearly to remove the speck from your brother's eye.

(Luke 6:37–42)

Questions for Biblical Reflection

1. In the first part of this text Jesus teaches us that when we close our hearts to others in judgment, condemnation, lack of forgiveness, or stinginess, we are also closing our hearts to receiving love. When we open our hearts to others in love and compassion, we open our hearts to *receive* love and compassion. Describe an example of how this has worked in your life.

_____

_____

_____

_____

_____

2. As you think about becoming willing to make amends, you may be aware of people whom you are judging or condemning. Write a short prayer acknowledging your feelings toward one such person and asking God to give you new eyes and a new heart to see this person with love.

_____

_____

_____

_____

_____

_____

3. Sometimes we have "blind spots" and are unable to see others through eyes of compassion. We may be blind to the value and worth of some of the people we have harmed. Often this kind of blindness is caused by unresolved guilt over harm we have done. As we become willing to make amends, some of this blindness will be removed. As you think about becoming willing to make amends to one of the people you have harmed, write a few sentences describing that person's value and worth in God's eyes:

_____

_____

_____

_____

_____

_____

4. Sometimes our "blindness" is a blindness to our own value and worth. This blindness can also interfere with our willingness to make amends. What would help you to see more clearly your own value and worth?

_____

_____

_____

_____

_____

_____

5. In the same way that we hurt others by judging them and condemning them, we hurt ourselves by judging and condemning ourselves. In what way do you judge or condemn yourself? What would help you turn these self-judgments over to God for his care?

_____

_____

_____

_____

_____

_____

6. Jesus asks, "Why do you look at the speck of sawdust in your brother's eye and pay no attention to the plank in your own eye?" Jesus is warning us against doing another person's inventory. Why is it so tempting to focus our attention on the "specks" in other people's eyes?

_____

_____

_____

_____

_____

7. What parts of Jesus' teaching in this text are especially helpful to you as you get ready to remove the "planks" from your eyes by becoming willing to make amends?

_____

_____

_____

_____

_____

▶ Step Eight in Action

1. **Make a list.** Use your Step Four inventory to help you make a list of the people you have harmed. Beside each name, list categories of possible harm such as economic, emotional, psychological, and spiritual. Within each category of possible harm list the specific events or behaviors that you belive were harmful.

2. **Become Willing to Make Amends.** Review your list. Think about each person on your list. Do not expect yourself to become willing to make amends to all of them all at once. Review your feelings toward each person. If you are angry with the person, you may not yet be willing to make amends. Talk to God about your anger, fear, and hurt. Ask God to show you the barriers that stand in the way of your willingness to make amends to each person. When you are willing to make amends to a particular person, make a note

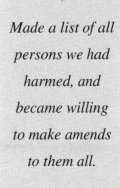

Made a list of all persons we had harmed, and became willing to make amends to them all.

of that on your list.

3. **Get support.** Finding support is an important part of becoming willing to make amends. Ask for God's help and the help of others in this process. We must do whatever it takes to build a supportive community of people who will encourage us in this process. Without support, it will be hard to sustain a willingness to make amends.

▶ ## Step Eight Prayer

Dear God,
I ask for help in making a list of the people I have harmed.
I want to take responsibility for my actions.
Grant me the willingness to make amends.
Amen.

Step 9

**Making
Amends**

*"You can't think your way into right living;
you have to live your way into right thinking."*

About Step Nine

There may be some wrongs we can never fully right. We don't
worry about them if we can honestly say to ourselves that we
would right them if we could. Some people cannot be seen—we
send them an honest letter. And there may be a valid reason for
postponement in some cases. But we don't delay if it can be
avoided. We should be sensible, tactful, considerate and humble
without being servile or scraping. As God's people we stand
on our feet; we don't crawl before anyone.
—Anonymous, *The Big Book of Alcoholics Anonymous*

For our continued recovery and spiritual well-being, our making
amends must in no way be contingent upon the other person's
response (except when to do so would injure him or her). We must
overlook the perceived injustices we have experienced as well as
see beyond the innumerable rationalizations we conceive to avoid
this step. We must shatter every excuse that hinders the taking of
this vital step in the path of recovery. What matters here is not what
we are owed, but rather what we owe! Though we cannot control
how our efforts at amends will be received by another,
this step of restoration remains life or death to us;
we must pay our pound though owed a million.
—Martin M. Davis, *The Gospel and the Twelve Steps*

Step 9

Making Amends

Step Nine suggests that after we have identified the people we have harmed and have taken time to adequately prepare ourselves, we actually make amends for the harm we have done:

Made direct amends to such people wherever possible except when to do so would injure them or others.

Our work in Step Eight provided us with a list of the people we have harmed. In Step Nine we make amends to the people on this list. Careful thought must be given to how we make each amend. Making amends involves more than just an apology. It involves a change in behavior. Apologizing—saying we are sorry—is a good thing to do. But it is only a part of making amends. When we make amends we do whatever we can to undo the harm we have done. If we have harmed someone emotionally, then we seek ways to undo that emotional damage. If we have harmed someone economically, then we seek ways to undo that economic damage. If we have harmed someone spiritually, then we seek ways to undo that spiritual damage. Our amends will be as diverse as the kinds of harm we have done to others.

For many of us, making amends may be a new—and sometimes uncomfortable—behavior. Most people, however, find that the process is a deeply rewarding experience.

► Step Nine: A Closer Look

Made Direct Amends

Direct amends are those we make to people whom we can contact personally. This includes family members, friends, creditors, coworkers and others. The kind of contact we make will vary from situation to situation. Meeting in person is the best way to make amends when this is possible. A letter or phone call is appropriate if a meeting is not possible. In some cases a personal meeting may be all that is required to complete the amends. In other cases, a personal meeting may be the beginning of a long process during which we seek to undo the damage we have done.

The importance of making amends is stated clearly in Scripture:

> *"When a man or woman wrongs another in any way and so is unfaithful to the LORD, that person is guilty and must confess the sin he has committed. He must make full restitution for his wrong, add one fifth to it and give it all to the person he has wronged." (Numbers 5:6, 7)*

Notice in this text that confession of sin is followed by full restitution for the harm done. The most fundamental reason for the biblical emphasis on making amends is that a passion for justice is part of God's character. Making amends is one way that we can bring about justice. The Bible frequently emphasizes that doing justice is even more important to God than any religious acts that we might perform: "To do what is right and just is more acceptable to the LORD than sacrifice" (Proverbs 21:3).

Wherever Possible

What if direct amends are not possible? A person we have harmed may have died, moved away, or for some other reason become unavailable to us. If that is the case, it doesn't mean we do nothing. If we caused economic harm to someone who has since died, we can still make restitution to his or her family. Or if that isn't possible, we can donate the money to an organization that might have been helpful to the deceased. The important thing is to find a way to undo the harm we have done—or at least to make it clear by our behavior that we would undo the harm if it were possible to do so. Step Nine recognizes that it is not always possible to make amends, but for our own sakes, we need to be creative and persistent in our efforts to make amends before we decide that a particular amend is not possible. Indirect amends and partial amends are appropriate when full, direct amends are not possible.

Except When to Do So Would Injure Them or Others

It is possible for amends to cause additional injury. In these situations, we must carefully consider how to make the amends. Sometimes the potential for additional harm will be obvious. Suppose you had a sexual affair with someone, but the spouse of that person is unaware of the affair. You have done harm to that spouse. This person needs to be on your amends list, but making direct amends could obviously cause additional harm to both parties, especially if the spouse does not know about the affair. Our need to make amends does not justify interfering with other people's relationships. Another kind of additional injury we need to be aware of is potential harm to ourselves. If the person on our list is actively abusive toward us and we have had to maintain strong boundaries to keep from being harmed, then making direct amends is probably unwise. If you are uncertain about what to do in a relationship that has been abusive, seek wise counsel before proceeding.

In addition to obvious kinds of additional harm, there are more subtle ways in which we can do harm by making amends. Suppose we go to a person we have harmed and say this: "I apologize for my part of the problem. I have confessed my sins, turned it over to God, and received God's forgiveness. Now to make progress in my recovery I need your forgiveness, and I'm asking you to forgive me." Can you hear the manipulative and controlling elements in this effort to make amends? It could easily communicate "I've done my part. Now it's up to you. You must forgive me or suffer the consequences." That sounds more like a threat than an amend! This kind of controlling behavior is another example of the way in which the poorly planned and premature making of amends can result in additional injury. We are *not* responsible for how people respond to our amends, but it is our responsibility to pay attention to the potential for additional injury that amends can cause. If we prepare ourselves poorly—or if seek to make amends before we have really "become willing"—then additional harm will result.

The bottom line is this: Step Nine invites us to develop *empathy*—the capacity to anticipate how others will be affected by our amends. This is exactly the quality of character that we lacked at the time that we did the harm we are now seeking to undo. The principle involved here is a biblical one: "Each of you should look not only to your own interests, but also to the interests of others" (Philippians 2:4).

Step Nine Bible Study

Questions for Personal Preparation

1. How prepared do you feel to make amends to the people on your list?

_____

_____

_____

_____

_____

2. What benefits do you hope will come from the process of making amends?

_____

_____

_____

_____

_____

Biblical Text

The text for this study comes from the teaching of Jesus on the subject of our relationships and the importance of making amends to people we have harmed.

> *"Therefore, if you are offering your gift at the altar and there remember that your brother has something against you, leave your gift there in front of the altar. First go and be reconciled to your brother; then come and offer your gift....You have heard that it was said, 'Love your neighbor and hate your enemy.' But I tell you: Love your enemies and pray for those who persecute you, that you may be sons of your Father in heaven. He causes his sun to rise on the evil and the good, and sends rain on the righteous and the unrighteous." (Matthew 5:23, 24, 43–45).*

Questions for Biblical Reflection

1. Jesus teaches that we cannot hurt other people and then worship God as if there were nothing wrong. Jesus insists that making amends is a matter of urgency to God. It is more urgent than any formal act of worship. Religious activities, such as worship, are less important to God than living lives that are honest and loving. Write whatever response you have to the value that Jesus places on making amends.

_____

_____

_____

_____

_____

_____

_____

2. The words of Jesus make it clear that God places a high value on love and honesty in our relationships. The importance of making amends to those we have harmed is one way to put into action this call to loving, honest relationships. Describe any ways in which the increased love and honesty you are developing by working the Twelve Steps have helped you to improve your relationships.

_____

_____

_____

_____

_____

_____

_____

3. How might it help you to think of making amends as an expression of love for God?

_____

_____

_____

_____

_____

_____

_____

4. How might it help you to think of making amends to someone as an expression of love for the person to whom you are making amends?

_____

_____

_____

_____

_____

5. In Step Eight we became ready to make amends to all people we have harmed, even to people who have harmed us. Jesus teaches in this text that we show God's love and kindness when we pray for and do good to our enemies—to those who have done harm to us. Is there anyone on your list you would consider an enemy, or toward whom you feel anger or resentment? Take a few minutes to pray for those people and for yourself in relationship to them. Write about your experience in this time of prayer.

_____

_____

_____

_____

_____

_____

6. Think of a time when someone made amends to you for a wrong done. What was the result, and how did you feel after the person made amends to you?

_____

_____

_____

_____

7. In a moment of quiet, picture yourself making amends to someone on your list. Picture God's presence there with you, giving you strength and courage. What images come to mind?

_____

_____

_____

_____

_____

Step Nine in Action

A comprehensive approach to Step Nine takes a long time. For this exercise, choose one person to whom you want to make amends. It is best to begin with amends that will be relatively easy to make. Be sure you are ready to make amends to this person. If you are not ready, you need to go back to Step Eight and work on getting ready. If you are ready to make amends to this person, then do the following.

Make plans.

Decide how, when, and where to make the amends. Try to keep your plans as simple as possible. Focus on the goal—to make amends. You are not trying to completely restore a relationship in one meeting. In many cases it is best to write out in advance exactly what you want to say to the person you have harmed. Include an acknowledgment that you have done harm, an expression of regret for your behavior, and an explanation of any restitution or changes you intend to make to help undo the harm you have done. Make sure that any changes you commit to are ones that you can actually do.

Made direct amends to such people wherever possible except when to do so would injure them or others.

Contact the person.

Contact the person to whom you want to make amends. Tell that person the truth: you have started to work a Twelve Step program and as part of that program you are seeking to meet with people you have harmed for the purpose of making amends. Request an opportunity to meet with that person.

Make the amends.

When you meet, read the statement you have prepared. It is important to keep the focus on your part of the problem. If the other person wants to talk about his or her part, it is that person's choice. But you need to stay focused on your own behaviors. For example, you might say: "I'm here because I want to make amends for [*the behavior that caused the harm*]. I know that I hurt you. I regret what I did. I am prepared to try to undo the harm I have done, as much as possible. Specifically, I would like to [*list actions, if any, you have planned*]. Thank you for listening to me. If you would like to respond, I will be happy to listen; if you do not want to respond, that's OK too."

Allow feedback.

The person to whom you are making amends may want to tell you his or her experience of the wrongs you have done. Healing happens as we receive feedback from someone we have harmed without slipping into past defensive behaviors. Listen attentively. It may not be easy, but listening may be the single most important way we can provide restitution. If we can listen without becoming defensive, we will be helping the healing process.

Talk with someone else.

When you have finished a meeting to make amends, talk with a trusted friend, therapist, or pastor, and share your experience. Acknowledge that it took courage for you to make the amends. Express any difficulties you had with the meeting. Finally, follow through with whatever commitments you have made to provide restitution.

► Step Nine Prayer

Dear God,
Give me the right attitude about making amends.
Help me to remember that
I am not doing this to change other people
but to make it possible for me to change.
Give me the hope I need.
Help me to remember that you have
shown your grace to me in many ways.
Give me the humility I need.
Help me to remember that I am a creature, not the Creator.
Give me the courage I need, God.
Help me to remember that your power within me
far exceeds the fear in front of me.
Amen.

Step 10

**Continuing
Inventory**

"Progress, Not Perfection."

About Step Ten

In the Steps which precede the Tenth, we have been dealing with the past—cleaning house, so to speak. We have searched the corners of memory for grievances to be adjusted by means of our new view of our role in life. Now, with Step Ten, this procedure becomes a daily ritual, a housecleaning that takes place in a nightly review of the day's happenings.
–Anonymous, *One Day At A Time in Al-Anon*

Working the steps is a daily struggle; the Christian walk is a daily struggle. These two manners of living are the same, a common path that must be walked one day at a time. The essential nature of the daily struggle is implied in Step Ten as we continue to implement the spiritual principles developed thus far. Jesus tells us to take up our cross daily and follow him (Luke 9:23). To take time away from the true path of recovery is to invite relapse and regression
into active addiction.
—Martin M. Davis, *The Gospel and the Twelve Steps*

▶ *Step 10* ◀

Continuing Inventory

The Twelve Steps are not a "cure" for anything. *The Big Book of Alcoholics Anonymous* makes a more modest claim for the Twelve Steps: "We are not cured of alcoholism. What we really have is a daily reprieve contingent on the maintenance of our spiritual condition." What is true for alcoholics is true for all of us: without continued efforts to maintain our spiritual condition we will return to our old way of life. Step Ten begins this maintenance part of the process:

Continued to take personal inventory and,
when we were wrong, promptly admitted it.

We use Step Ten to preserve our progress by reviewing our actions on a daily basis. We need to be patient with this process—and patient with ourselves. In Step Ten we develop a daily discipline of reflecting on the events of our day and making note of things that need corrective action. When we identify behaviors that were inappropriate, we take corrective action as soon as possible. Step Ten, in essence, is an abbreviated version of Steps Four through Nine, done daily. When done regularly, the continual inventory in Step Ten can help us develop a day-at-a-time lifestyle and provide us with a daily reprieve from our old ways of life.

▶ Step Ten: A Closer Look

Continued

Step Ten encourages us to practice the spiritual disciplines of the Twelve Steps on a daily basis. Most of us would prefer to be healed permanently with no need to "continue" on a daily basis. All of us experience our healing as taking longer than we would prefer. But the behaviors we want to change have been with us for a long time, and change does not usually come quickly. It may be painful and sometimes embarrassing to admit that the same old issues keep resurfacing over and over again. But continuing to take our personal inventory keeps us honest—and humble. Patience may not be our favorite virtue, but it is essential for the healing process:

A patient man has great understanding,
but a quick-tempered man displays folly. (Proverbs 14:29)

An alternative to patience is pretense. But if we try to pretend that we don't need to continue the work we have started, we are deceiving ourselves:

> *If we claim to be without sin, we deceive ourselves and the truth is not in us. If we confess our sins, he is faithful and just and will forgive us our sins and purify us from all unrighteousness. If we claim we have not sinned, we make him out to be a liar and his word has no place in our lives. (1 John 1:8-10)*

To Take Personal Inventory

The purpose of a daily inventory is to help us develop a disciplined program that includes the examination of conscience, confession, and making amends. These disciplines become part of the basic structure of our lives. By now we have used the spiritual disciplines of the Twelve Steps long enough to recognize that we easily retreat into old patterns of behavior. We forget easily. It's like looking into a mirror and then turning away. It takes only a few minutes to forget what we saw.

> *Anyone who listens to the word but does not do what it says is like a man who looks at his face in a mirror and, after looking at himself, goes away and immediately forgets what he looks like." (James 1:23, 24)*

Step Ten offers a daily look into our spiritual mirror. When we find things that need to be changed, we make note of them and take action promptly. Taking a regular inventory of our activities helps us to see how we are behaving. If we are obsessing about things again, comparing ourselves to others, trying to control things, or engaging in other types of old behavior, our daily inventory warns us that we are reverting to old patterns.

The advantage of continuing to take an inventory on a daily basis is that we will be able to see our mistakes before we have a major relapse. In A.A. you sometimes hear the slogan that makes that point: "Relapse starts long before the drink is drunk." A regular inventory can also help us to identify areas where we are developing new strengths as God responds to our Step Seven prayer to remove our shortcomings. Our regular inventory should include a record of these signs that God is changing us.

And When We Were Wrong, Promptly Admitted It

There will be times when we will be wrong. We are fallible human beings, and we can expect to make mistakes. We need to realize that we will experience failure and lapse into old behavior patterns. Step Ten suggests that, when we recognize our wrongs, we promptly admit them. It is this simple spiritual humility that will save us from falling into the downward spiral of relapse.

Promptness in admitting our wrongs is important. One of the things we identified in Steps Eight and Nine is that postponed amends become much more complicated and difficult to make. We know from experience that holding on to anger and resentment is counterproductive and can be harmful to our physical and mental well-being. The quicker we resolve issues, the quicker we will find relief. Jesus tells us, "Settle matters quickly with your adversary who is taking you to court. Do it while you are still with him on the way [to court]" (Matthew 5:25).

▶ ## Step Ten Bible Study

Questions for Personal Preparation

1. When you become aware that your actions are harmful to yourself or others, how do you usually respond?

_____

_____

_____

_____

_____

_____

_____

2. How would you like to respond?

_____

_____

_____

_____

_____

_____

_____

Biblical Text

In the text for this study, a short selection from an ancient hymn, the psalmist prays for God's help as he continues the process of learning about himself.

> *O LORD, you have searched me and you know me. You know when I sit and when I rise; you perceive my thoughts from afar. You discern my going out and my lying down; you are familiar with all my ways. Before a word is on my tongue you know it completely, O LORD. You hem me in— behind and before; you have laid your hand upon me. Such knowledge is too wonderful for me, too lofty for me to attain. Where can I go from your Spirit? Where can I flee from your presence? If I go up to the heavens, you are there; if I make my bed in the depths, you are there. If I rise on the wings of the dawn, if I settle on the far side of the sea, even there your hand will guide me, your right hand will hold me fast....*
>
> *Search me, O God, and know my heart; test me and know my anxious thoughts. See if there is any offensive way in me, and lead me in the way everlasting.*
>
> *(Psalm 139:1–10, 23, 24)*

1. In the first part of this text, the psalmist expresses gratitude to God for God's attentive, loving presence in his life. He is saying, "God you know me intimately. You pay attention to me. You are always with me, and you hold me in your hands." How might a daily awareness of God's presence help you to continue to take a regular inventory and to promptly admit your wrongs?

_____

_____

_____

_____

2. What positive changes in your behavior have resulted from your work in Steps Four and Five?

_____

_____

_____

_____

3. What positive changes in your relationships have resulted from your work in Steps Eight and Nine?

_____

_____

_____

_____

_____

4. Because God knows us better than we know ourselves, we can ask God to help us with our ongoing inventory, just as we have asked for help in the other Steps. The psalmist first asks God to search his heart. In our hearts are our deepest longings, hopes, and desires. Take a few minutes to ask God to search your heart and to reveal what is there. Write whatever God reveals to you.

_____

_____

_____

_____

_____

5. The psalmist then asks God to know his anxious thoughts. Ask God to reveal your anxious thoughts. Write whatever God reveals to you.

_____

_____

_____

_____

_____

6. The psalmist then asks God to see if there is any offensive way in him. Ask God to reveal your offensive ways. Write whatever God reveals to you.

_____

_____

_____

_____

7. Review your answers to questions 4, 5, and 6. List any wrongs you need to admit to God, to yourself, and to another human being.

_____

_____

_____

_____

_____

_____

_____

▶ Step Ten in Action

Step Ten helps us to be aware of our behavior and alerts us when old patterns of behavior have returned. When old, harmful behaviors appear, prompt corrective action is necessary. If you are just starting to work on Step Ten, we suggest you try the following:

1. Set a specific time each day to work on Step Ten.
If you are a "morning person," plan to work on Step Ten in the morning. It is best to choose a time when you have the energy and ability to focus. It is also usually best to use the same time each day, if possible. Plan to spend ten to fifteen minutes each day for your daily inventory.

2. Prepare yourself.
Begin by asking God to quiet your heart and mind. Be aware of his loving and grace-full presence. Ask God to help you open your heart and mind to whatever he chooses to reveal to you.

3. Write.
Write about your thoughts, fears, resentments, and behaviors during the past twenty-four hours. It is best to have a journal for this purpose. Include any observations you've made about how God is removing your defects of character.

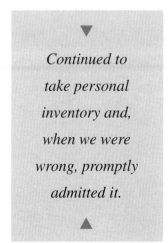

Continued to take personal inventory and, when we were wrong, promptly admitted it.

4. Express gratitude.

Thank God for helping you continue to take personal inventory and for guiding you to make positive changes in your life. Thank God for your new ability to admit your wrongs and to promptly correct them.

5. Take Action.

Admit to yourself and to God any wrongs that you observe. Also admit them to another person.

As you gain more experience with Step Ten you will develop a routine that works best for you. How you do it is not as important as doing it.

Step Ten Prayer

Dear God,
Help me to continue what has been started.
To grow in understanding,
To take daily inventories of life,
To correct mistakes when I make them,
To take responsibility for my actions,
To be aware of my self-defeating thoughts and behaviors,
To always remember that I need your help,
To be loving and tolerant of myself and others, and
To continue in daily prayer.
Amen.

Step 11

**Seeking
God**

*"You can't direct the wind,
but you can adjust your sails."*

About Step Eleven

As we go through the day we pause, when agitated or doubtful,
and ask for the right thought or action. We constantly remind
ourselves we are no longer running the show, humbly saying to
ourselves many times each day "Thy will be done." We are then
in much less danger of excitement, fear, anger, worry, self-pity
or foolish decisions. We become much more efficient. We do
not tire as easily, for we are not burning up energy foolishly as
we did when we were trying to arrange life to suit ourselves.
—Anonymous, *The Big Book of Alcoholics Anonymous*

Those of us who have come to make regular use of prayer
would no more do without it than we would refuse air, food or
sunshine. And for the same reason. When we refuse air, light,
or food, the body suffers. And when we turn away from meditation and prayer, we likewise deprive our minds, our emotions,
and our intuitions of vitally needed support. As the body can
fail its purpose for lack of nourishment, so can the soul.
—Anonymous, *Twelve Steps and Twelve Traditions*

Step 11

Seeking God

S teps Ten and Eleven are often referred to as the "maintenance" Steps, because they help us to sustain the progress we have made in Steps One through Nine. In Step Ten we learned the value of continuing to practice honest self-examination through regular inventory and confession. In Step Eleven we seek to improve our conscious contact with God and we pray for his will to be done in our lives:

Sought through prayer and meditation
to improve our conscious contact with God as we understood Him,
praying only for knowledge of His will for us
and the power to carry that out.

As we review the work we have done so far, we can see signs that our spiritual lives have already undergone significant changes. Many of us had a very troubled relationship with God when we started using the Twelve Steps. We may not have trusted God or wanted anything to do with him. Our spiritual transformation began in Steps Two and Three, when we came to believe that a Power greater than ourselves could restore us to sanity and then made a decision to turn our lives over to God's care. In Steps Four through Seven we learned that God is there to help us with our shortcomings—not to abandon or reject us because of them. Throughout our journey of working the Steps we have turned to God for help and strength. Now, in Step Eleven, we focus directly on God, as we seek to increase our conscious contact with him and pray for the knowledge of his will for our lives.

▶ Step Eleven: A Closer Look

Sought Through Prayer

There are many types of prayer. Prayer can be intimate conversation with our Creator—a conversation that begins with God's invitation to us. God says to us: "Call upon me in the day of trouble; I will deliver you, and you will honor me" (Psalm 50:15). Prayer can be a means of sharing our lives with God in a way that makes us aware of God's loving presence with us. In Step Eleven we use a specific kind of prayer. We ask for three very specific things. We pray for improvement in our conscious contact with God, for knowledge of God's will, and for the power to carry out God's will. We do not seek though prayer to control the details of our lives—or the lives of others. We do not seek through prayer to have things our way.

And Meditation

Meditation is a spiritual discipline that dates back to biblical times. Meditation makes possible a kind of intentional and deeply personal connection with God. The experience of meditation will not always be the same. For example, during a difficult period in his life, the psalmist prayed: "I remembered you, O God, and I groaned; I mused [meditated], and my spirit grew faint" (Psalm 77:3). But meditation can also be a joyful experience. The psalmist also wrote: "May my meditation be pleasing to him, as I rejoice in the LORD" (Psalm 104:34).

The kind of meditation we find in Step Eleven focuses on waiting and listening for God in order to learn his will for us. The prophet Isaiah talked about this "waiting" kind of meditation when he prayed, "Yes, LORD, walking in the way of your laws, we wait for you; your name and renown are the desire of our hearts" (Isaiah 26:8). This kind of meditation is a way to listen to what God has to say. The psalmist suggests that we "be still before the LORD and wait patiently for him" (Psalm 37:7). In meditation we wait patiently and we listen. We quiet our hearts and minds so that we can listen.

To Improve Our Conscious Contact with God

Improving our conscious contact with God means that we seek to deepen our experience of God and to recognize God's presence in our lives on a more regular basis. As we look back over the work we have done in spiritual kindergarten, we can see signs that our conscious contact with God is already improving. When we started our journey in spiritual kindergarten, most of us reached out to God out of desperation. Now we turn to God not so much out of desperation but out of a desire to know him better. God has already helped us, and it is normal to want to know more about this Higher Power that has been so helpful. As we discover how much God loves us, we will draw near to him because of the joy we experience in his presence.

When we develop a routine of seeking God's will for us, our ability to experience God's presence in our lives will increase. We know that God is always with us, but we are often blinded to his presence. The more time we are able to spend in conscious contact with God, the more we will be able to "see" God—to experience God's presence in the ordinary events of our daily lives. As we work on Step Eleven we will find ourselves saying with the psalmist, "The LORD sets prisoners free, the LORD gives sight to the blind" (Psalm 146:7, 8).

As We Understood Him

This phrase is the same as we found in Step Three. In Step Three we noted that this phrase was not intended to imply that our understanding about God was very complete. It was intended only to suggest that we were to proceed on the basis of what we had learned in Step Two. We can now look back and see more clearly the truth of this. Our understanding of God then was quite different from what it is today. We have now seen God's power to help us. We are growing spiritually. Our relationship with God is changing. Our understanding—our experience—of God is not stagnant. This is very good news! The phrase "as we understood Him" in Step Eleven is another reminder that the Twelve Steps are a spiritual kindergarten. We are seeking to improve our conscious contact with God because we know that our understanding of God is still incomplete. Here in spiritual kindergarten we need to be reminded again and again that our focus is to build our personal conscious contact with God. Our goal is not just to learn more *about* God; our goal is to be in conscious contact *with* God.

Praying Only for Knowledge of His Will for Us

Step Eleven is quite specific about the kind of prayer that is appropriate for us. We are to pray *only* for knowledge of God's will and for the power to carry it out. This is quite different from the way many of us are accustomed to praying. We may have prayed: "Oh, God, don't let me get caught!" or "God, please fix my spouse so that I can be happy." Some of us even prayed to be freed from our problems so that we could continue to act in the same way without any consequences! In these and many other ways we have used prayer as a tool to manipulate God. We wanted God to answer our prayers according to *our* wills and to increase our power so that we could carry out *our* wills. This kind of prayer is part of the problem.

In Step Eleven we learn a completely different approach to prayer. We pray to know God's will, not for God to know *our* wills. The first ten Steps have taught us that we are not wise enough or powerful enough to come up with an appropriate agenda for God to carry out. In Step Eleven we learn to pray for knowledge of *God's* will and the power to carry it out. This helps us remember that God is in charge, and it is our responsibility to align ourselves with his will. God's agenda is what we need to seek and to follow. The Apostle Paul put it like this: "Do not conform any longer to the pattern of this world, but be transformed by the renewing of your mind. Then you will be able to test and approve what God's will is—his good, pleasing and perfect will" (Romans 12:2).

And the Power to Carry That Out

In Step Eleven we pray for power to do God's will. We are not asking for a recharge of our batteries, so that we can keep on trying harder to do things according to our agenda. No recharging of our batteries will give us the power we need. We learned in Step One that we are powerless to do what needs to be done. In Step Two we learned that God is more powerful than we are. The power to do God's will must come from God.

God has a long history of demonstrating his power through the weakness of his people. Most of us would certainly prefer that God use our strengths, our gifted-ness, our abilities—or that he make us stronger, more gifted, more able. But it is our weakness that God uses to demonstrate his power. God tells us: "My grace is sufficient for you, for my power is made perfect in weakness" (2 Corinthians 12:9). We pray for power to carry out God's will. But God chooses to empower us in surprising ways. In the vulnerability of confession we see God's power at work, transforming our hearts. In the humility of making amends we see God's power at work, transforming our lives. The slogan "Let go and let God" captures what is important here. Letting go does not usually leave us feeling powerful; it usually leaves us feeling vulnerable. But it is only in the vulnerability of letting go that we are able to let God's powerful and loving will be at the center of our lives.

► Step Eleven Bible Study

Questions for Personal Preparation

1. What is your current experience of prayer? Has it been a helpful part of your spiritual journey?

_____

_____

_____

_____

2. What is your current experience of meditation? How has God reached you in moments of quiet reflection?

_____

_____

_____

_____

_____

Biblical Text

The text for this study is part of Psalm 143. The psalmist expresses many of the things we commonly experience as part of Step Eleven.

> *Answer me quickly, O LORD; my spirit fails.*
> *Do not hide your face from me*
> *or I will be like those who go down to the pit.*
> *Let the morning bring me word of your unfailing love,*
> *for I have put my trust in you.*
> *Show me the way I should go, for to you I lift up my soul.*
> *Rescue me from my enemies, O LORD, for I hide myself in you.*
> *Teach me to do your will, for you are my God;*
> *may your good Spirit lead me on level ground.*
> *For your name's sake, O LORD, preserve my life;*
> *in your righteousness, bring me out of trouble.*
> *(Psalm 143: 7–11)*

Questions for Biblical Reflection

1. Which of the psalmist's statements show his desire for improved conscious contact with God?

_____

_____

_____

_____

_____

_____

_____

2. Which of his statements describe the psalmist's desire to know God's will?

_____

_____

_____

_____

_____

3. Describe the changes you have seen in your relationship with God since you started working on the Twelve Steps.

_____

_____

_____

_____

_____

_____

4. Describe a time since you started using the Twelve Steps when God revealed his will to you and gave you the strength to carry it out.

_____

_____

_____

_____

_____

_____

5. What forms of prayer and meditation are the most helpful to you in improving your conscious contact with God and in seeking to know his will for you?

_____

_____

_____

_____

_____

6. Write a short prayer expressing to God your desire to improve your conscious contact with him.

_____

_____

_____

_____

_____

7. Write a short prayer expressing to God your desire to know and to follow his will.

_____

_____

_____

_____

_____

_____

Step Eleven in Action

There are many ways to seek improvements in our conscious contact with God through prayer and meditation. Here are several possibilities that might help you put Step Eleven into action.

Sought through prayer and meditation to improve our conscious contact with God as we understood Him, praying only for knowledge of His will for us and the power to carry that out.

1. Keep a prayer journal. Write a prayer to God every day. Include your daily inventory. Ask God to continue helping you to know areas in your life that need correcting. Ask for help in knowing and doing God's will in your life. After writing each prayer, remain quiet and listen for God's response. Spend a few minutes in silence, and be aware of God's loving presence. Don't be concerned if the answer doesn't come immediately. Sometimes God takes longer than we want, but the answer will come in God's time. Whether or not you sense a response from God, continue to be open to God's words or direction to you during the day. When you do sense God responding to you, write down what you sense God is saying to you.

2. Develop a method to remind yourself that God is present with you throughout the day. You can take a short "prayer break," or you can say a simple prayer many times during the day—for example, "Thank you for being with me, Lord," or "Teach me your loving ways, God." Whenever you need God's help, you can simply say, "God, I need some help."

3. Begin or end each day by making a gratitude list, thanking God for his many gifts to you throughout the day.

4. Read a psalm as part of your daily routine of inventory, prayer, and meditation. Spend time meditating on any part of the psalm that relates to your personal situation.

Remember that there is no right or wrong way to pray and meditate. These are tools to help you in your desire to improve your conscious contact with God and to understand his will for your life.

▶ Step Eleven Prayer

Dear God,
I seek to know you better.
I want to be conscious of your love.
I want to sense your presence with me.
I seek to know your will.
And I seek the power to carry it out.
Amen.

Step 12

Carrying
the Message

"You have to give it away in order to keep it."

About Step Twelve

Practical experience shows that nothing will so much insure immunity from drinking as intensive work with other alcoholics. It works when other activities fail. This is our twelfth suggestion: Carry this message to other alcoholics.
–Anonymous, *The Big Book of Alcoholics Anonymous*

When a man or a woman has a spiritual awakening, the most important meaning of it is that he has now become able to do, feel and believe that which he could not do before on his unaided strength and resources alone. He has been granted a gift which amounts to a new state of consciousness and being. He has been set on a path which tells him he is really going somewhere, that life is not a dead end, not something to be endured or mastered. In a very real sense he has been transformed, because he has laid hold of a source of strength which, in one way or another, he had hitherto denied himself. He finds himself in possession of a degree of honesty, tolerance, unselfishness, peace of mind, and love of which he had thought himself quite incapable. What he has received is a free gift, and yet usually, at least in some small part, he has made himself ready to receive it.
–Anonymous, *Twelve Steps and Twelve Traditions*

►*Step 12*◄

Carrying the Message

The first nine Steps taught us some basic skills about how to have a peaceful relationship with God, with ourselves, and with other people. In Steps Ten and Eleven we learned how to maintain peace in these relationships by the daily practice of our new skills. Now, in Step Twelve, we acknowledge that we have had a spiritual awakening as a result of working the Steps:

> *Having had a spiritual awakening as the result of these steps,*
> *we tried to carry this message to others and*
> *to practice these principles in all our affairs.*

We have learned a lot since we began using the Twelve Steps as our spiritual kindergarten. We have faced many painful realities about ourselves. We have learned to accept help and to tell the truth. We are now able to take responsibility for our actions and to stop blaming others for our deficiencies. Most significantly, we have discovered a Power greater than ourselves who loves us and who will restore us, care for us, change us, and guide us as we continue to turn our lives over to his care.

Step Twelve is the last Step—but nothing is coming to an end. On the contrary, we will continue to practice these new principles for the rest of our lives. As we continue to grow in our conscious contact with God, we will find that we have more joy, peace, and serenity in our lives. Remember that the Twelve Steps are a spiritual kindergarten—a way to begin our spiritual journey. If kindergarten can be this rich and rewarding, imagine what elementary school might be like! God is not done with us yet. The journey has just begun!

► Step Twelve: A Closer Look

Having Had a Spiritual Awakening
The primary change that the Twelve Steps make possible is a spiritual awakening. Many of us have been asleep—spiritually asleep. Now we are waking up. We are more alert, and we can see some remarkable changes in our attitude and behavior. It is not important to define precisely when or how we have had a spiritual awak-

ening, or even what words we could use to describe it. Our task is simply to acknowledge, with gratitude and humility, that we have experienced an awakening. We were asleep. Now we are waking up. The Apostle Paul used very similar language to describe what is needed: "The hour has come for you to wake up from your slumber....The night is nearly over; the day is almost here" (Romans 13:11, 12). It is good to be waking up!

As the Result of These Steps

The spiritual awakening we are experiencing happens as the result of working the Steps. A spiritual awakening is not the same for everyone. It happens at different times and in different ways. Some of us experience it early in the Steps when we realize how desperate we are for God's help. Others of us may have had an awakening in Step Four when we first made our inventory. Still others of us experience a spiritual awakening when in Step Nine we sense God's presence and power through each amend we make. For others it is not until we focus in Step Eleven on improving our conscious contact with God that we start to see ourselves wake up spiritually. Awakening from spiritual sleep is a long process for most of us. But it is a rewarding and exciting part of the journey.

We Tried to Carry This Message to Others

Carrying the message of our spiritual awakening to others is essential to our long-term health. Without sharing what we have received, we will be unable to keep what we have received. There is a lot of truth to the old slogan "You can only keep what you give away." When we share the message of our spiritual awakening with others, we are witnessing to the reality of God's healing power and to the way it has changed our lives. Jesus put it this way: "Let your light shine before men, that they may see your good deeds and praise your Father in heaven" (Matthew 5:16).

Before carrying the message to others, we need to be comfortable with our own progress in working the Steps. If we do not see positive changes in our own behavior and are not practicing the principles of the Steps in our daily affairs, our message will not be effective. In A.A. they say, "You gotta walk the walk before you talk the talk." If we don't "walk like we talk," what we share with others won't have any credibility. Telling the truth with rigorous honesty is essential when sharing our story with others. Our message needs to be a sincere testimony of our own experience, strength, and hope. We will carry the message more effectively if we stay closely connected with our own story; we dare not forget where we were when we started on this journey! If we forget our own history, we run the risk of losing compassion and sympathy for those who listen to our story. We must remember that we once were suffering, just as others are suffering today.

And to Practice These Principles in All Our Affairs

The principles of the Twelve Steps can be applied to every area of our lives. As we practice these principles in all our affairs, they will become an integral part of our lives. The important word here is "practice." We need to *do* what needs to be done. The Apostle Paul made the same point about spiritual growth: "Whatever you have learned or received or heard from me, or seen in me—put it into practice" (Philippians 4:9). James makes the same point: "Do not merely listen to the word, and so deceive yourselves. Do what it says" (James 1:22).

▶ Step Twelve Bible Study

Questions for Personal Preparation

1. Who "carried the message" of God's love and healing power to you? How was it conveyed, and what was your initial reaction to hearing the message?

_____

_____

_____

_____

_____

_____

2. Identify a situation where you carried the message to another person. How did you do this?

_____

_____

_____

_____

_____

_____

_____

_____

Biblical Text

It is God's intention that his people "carry the message" to others. In this text, the Apostle Paul, one of the leaders of the early church, talks about God's invitation to us to "carry the message."

> *Therefore, if anyone is in Christ, he is a new creation; the old has gone, the new has come! All this is from God, who reconciled us to himself through Christ and gave us the ministry of reconciliation: that God was reconciling the world to himself in Christ, not counting men's sins against them. And he has committed to us the message of reconciliation. We are therefore Christ's ambassadors, as though God were making his appeal through us. We implore you on Christ's behalf: Be reconciled to God.*
>
> *(2 Corinthians 5:17–20)*

Questions for Biblical Reflection

1. The text says that in Christ we are a new creation—"the old has gone, the new has come!" Give an example of how God is making you a "new creation."

_____

_____

_____

2. What "old" ways has God been removing from your life?

_____

_____

_____

_____

3. What would it mean to practice what you have learned from the Twelve Steps in all of your affairs? List specific examples of how this has been happening or how it might happen.

_____

_____

_____

_____

4. This text calls us to be reconciled to God and to carry the message of reconciliation to others. To *reconcile* is to restore harmony. The Twelve Steps bring us into better harmony with God, with ourselves, and with others. Write a brief description of your spiritual awakening—of your restored harmony with God, yourself, and others.

_____

_____

_____

_____

_____

_____

5. How can you share the experience of your spiritual awakening with others?

_____

_____

_____

_____

6. What barriers stand in the way of your doing this?

_____

_____

_____

_____

_____

7. How will sharing the message with others help you to continue to heal and change?

_____

_____

_____

_____

_____

Step Twelve in Action

The actions for Step Twelve involve "carrying the message to others" and "practicing the principles in all of our affairs."

1. Develop a specific plan to share the story of what God has done for you with one person.

2. Identify a situation in your life that is currently causing you concern and creating problems for you. Apply the principles of the Twelve Steps to that problem area. Begin with an admission of powerlessness over the problem, and continue through each of the Steps. When you have finished, review what you did, and describe how using the Twelve Steps helped you to resolve the problem.

Having had a spiritual awakening as the result of these steps, we tried to carry this message to others and to practice these principles in all our affairs.

Step Twelve Prayer

Dear God,
I was asleep.
Now I am waking up.
How wonderful it is to wake up to you!
Your presence brings such joy to my life.
Your love gives me such stability.
Your peace gives me such serenity.
I humbly pray for the ability
to share with others the story of what you have done.
I pray for the inner strength and wisdom
to practice the principles of this way of life
in all that I do and say.
Amen.

Resources for Group Leaders

We hope that you will consider doing the Bible studies in this book with a group. The dynamics of a group can add a lot to your personal journey! If you have led or participated in group Bible studies in the past, however, it will be important to remember that there are some significant differences between these Bible studies and more traditional Bible studies.

Traditional Bible study groups are really *discussion* groups. In such groups people share their ideas, discuss various perspectives, ask other people questions to clarify what they mean, and so on. There is nothing wrong with discussion groups; discussions can be valuable and helpful.
And you could in fact have a discussion group using these Bible studies. We encourage you, however, to consider introducing some of the customs and practices that have developed in the Twelve Step tradition as part of your Bible study group.

The customs and practices of Twelve Step groups are dramatically different from those commonly found in Bible study or discussion groups. In Twelve Step groups, discussion—often called "cross talk"—is typically forbidden. No efforts are made to "draw people out" or to "follow up on something someone has said" or to "ask people to clarify." Instead of *discussion,* Twelve Step groups emphasize *testimony.* The testimony format involves putting part of your story into words in such a way as to clarify how you have (or have not) experienced God to be at work. Like confession, testimony is a spiritual discipline that builds a capacity for telling the truth. Twelve Step groups spend most of the group's time allowing group members to tell their stories. It is a simple but very powerful dynamic. We think you will get the most benefit from these particular Bible studies if you follow the traditions of Twelve Step groups and make testimony the central purpose of your group meetings.

There is another difference between Twelve Step groups and traditional Bible study groups. You may have been in a Bible study group that began with a "safe" question, like "What's your favorite flavor of ice cream?" The theory is that, in order to build trust, you must begin with safe questions that don't involve much self-disclosure and then very gradually work toward questions that require increased amounts of self-disclosure. This is probably a reasonable approach for discussion-based small groups. The traditions of Twelve Step groups are, however, almost exactly the opposite of typical Bible studies and other small groups in the Christian community. Twelve Step groups typically begin by having participants say aloud one of the most difficult and painful facts of their lives. In some Twelve Step groups the first thing people say is typically "Hi! My name is ____, and I'm a _____." No attempt is made to gradually work up to "I'm a sex addict" or "I'm a cocaine addict." Such confession is an entry-level requirement for group participation in Twelve Step groups. While it may not be possible for your group to use the same self-introduction process used in Twelve Step groups, we encourage you to find some way to make confession a foundation for your group.

A third important distinctive of Twelve Step groups that needs to be emphasized has to do with the role of the group leader. Typical expectations of group leaders in traditional Bible studies is that they will be prepared to "teach" the group; they will have studied the text and maybe even come up with some creative questions or exercises or ideas. In Twelve Step groups the role of the leader is much less demanding. Most Twelve Step groups use a written "script" that the leader reads with little, if any, commentary or creativity. The main purpose of using a script is to ensure that the focus stays on testimony. Leaders of Twelve Step groups do not "teach" the group. Leaders are there to model honest testimony. We encourage you to find ways to keep testimony at the center of the life of your group!

The following sample group format may help you as you design a process for your group. It may take some effort to adapt it to your particular situation.

Format for a Twelve Step Group Bible Study

WELCOME

"Hello, and welcome to the Twelve Step Bible Study. My name is _____, and it is my turn to lead the meeting tonight. Please join me for a moment of silence, after which we will recite the Serenity Prayer."

God, grant me the serenity to accept the things I cannot change,
the courage to change the things I can,
and the wisdom to know the difference.

OPENING COMMENTS

"This group is committed to creating a safe place for us to share our experiences, strength, and hope. This is not a therapy group; no one is here in a professional capacity. Our purpose is to grow spiritually—to grow in our relationship with God. We are not here to talk about others, to condemn, criticize, or judge anyone. Our desire is to improve the quality of our lives by looking honestly at who we are, by learning from, listening to, and sharing with each other, by placing ourselves in the care of our Higher Power, Jesus Christ, and by engaging in healthier behaviors. This group is sponsored by _____ (church or organization name, if any) as a way to introduce people to Christ-centered recovery. There are various other groups and courses of study offered throughout the year. A calendar that lists options available to you is on the literature table."

THE TWELVE STEPS

"The spiritual disciplines of the Twelve Steps are an important foundation for our group, so I've asked _____ to read the Twelve Steps for us. And after each step is read, I've asked _____ to read a biblical text that helps to clarify the meaning of that step."

ANNOUNCEMENTS

"Are there any recovery-related announcements?"

NEWCOMERS

"Is there anyone here today for the first time? If so, please tell us your first name so we can greet you. If you are new to a Twelve Step support group, we offer you a special welcome. We suggest that you attend at least six meetings to give yourself a fair chance to decide if this group is appropriate for you. If you have any questions, please feel free to talk with me at the end of the meeting."

INTRODUCTIONS

"It is our custom to introduce ourselves by first name only. If you would like to identify your primary problem as part of introducing yourself, we welcome you to do so. Please do not feel compelled, however, to introduce yourself other than to share your first name. My name is _____, and I'm a recovering _____." (Note: The custom in most Twelve Step groups is to respond to each person's self-introduction by saying "Hi, [name of the person]!")

GROUP GUIDELINES

"At every meeting we remind ourselves of some basic group guidelines. Many of the principles and traditions of Alcoholics Anonymous are used as part of our group. We respect the confidentiality and anonymity of each person here. Remember that whatever you hear at this meeting is shared with the trust and confidence that it will remain here. 'Who you see here, what is said here, when you leave here, let it stay here.' Before our sharing begins, I will read our Guidelines for Group Sharing."

GUIDELINES FOR GROUP SHARING

1. Everyone is invited to share, but no one is obligated to do so.
2. Please keep your sharing focused on recent experiences and events. Focus on your personal experience, strength, and hope.
3. Limit your sharing to three to five minutes. Allow everyone in the group to share once before you share a second time.
4. Please, NO CROSS TALK. Cross talk occurs when people speak out of turn or interrupt another person. The group is disrupted, and focus is diverted from the individual whose turn it is to speak.
5. Please refrain from asking questions. Questions will be answered after the meeting so that sharing will not be interrupted.
6. If you have recently used chemical substances that have had a mood-altering effect on you, we ask you not to share until after the meeting.
7. We are not here to advise, soothe, or solve other people's problems. We can share what we have done to change our own behavior, but not what we think someone else should do.

SHARING

"This meeting is a Bible study–based meeting related to one of the Twelve Steps. The Twelve Steps can provide a way out of destructive behavior and an opportunity to improve our relationship with God. The study for tonight's meeting is related to Step _____. I have asked _____ to read the biblical text for today's study, which is found in _____[biblical reference]."

"As your leader for this meeting, I will share for a few minutes, and then I will open the meeting for general sharing of your experience, strength, and hope. Please limit yourself to comments about your *experience* of working on the Step for this week, the *strength* you are gaining by working on this Step, and the *hope* that this Step is making possible for you. If you have not worked through this study prior to our group meeting, I encourage you to listen to the comments of others before taking a turn. If you would like to share, please raise your hand to be recognized."

(Note: After sharing personally, the leader gives others an opportunity to speak from their experiences. If the group is larger than twenty people, many groups will form smaller groups of five to seven people for the sharing portion of the meeting.)

PRAYER

"We will now take time for prayer requests. These requests should be regarding yourself or other group members." (Note: A time of prayer follows. The prayer time can be structured in a variety of ways, depending on the customs of the group.)

CLOSING

"This Bible study is a fellowship of _____ (church or organization name) and is intended to complement, not replace, other Twelve Step groups. We encourage you to attend other Twelve Step meetings that apply to your situation. We also encourage you to bring a friend to this group or to other Twelve Step groups and to invite them to experience some of the benefits that can be gained from participating in this program. Remember: What you hear at this meeting is confidential; leave it at this meeting! It is not for public disclosure or gossip. Please respect the privacy of those who have shared here today. Will all who care to, stand, join hands, and join me in closing with the Lord's Prayer?"

Our Father which art in heaven,
Hallowed be thy name.
Thy kingdom come. Thy will be done in earth, as it is in heaven.
Give us this day our daily bread.
And forgive us our debts, as we forgive our debtors.
And lead us not into temptation, but deliver us from evil:
For thine is the kingdom,
and the power, and the glory, for ever. Amen.
(Matthew 6:9–13, KJV)

"KEEP COMING BACK. IT WORKS!"

(Note: In many groups this is commonly said in unison after the end of the Lord's Prayer.)

The Twelve Steps

LEARNING TO LIVE IN PEACE WITH GOD

1 We admitted we were powerless over _____–that our lives had become unmanageable.

For I have the desire to do what is good, but I cannot carry it out.
Romans 7:18

2 Came to believe that a power greater than ourselves could restore us to sanity

The LORD is my shepherd, I shall not be in want. He makes me lie down in green pastures, he leads me beside quiet waters, he restores my soul.
Psalm 23:1-3

3 Made a decision to turn our will and our lives over to the care of God as we understood him.

I have set before you life and death, blessings and curses. Now choose life, so that you and your children may live and that you may love the LORD your God, listen to his voice, and hold fast to him.
Deuteronomy 30:19-20

LEARNING TO LIVE IN PEACE WITH OURSELVES

4 Made a searching and fearless moral inventory of ourselves.

Let us examine our ways and test them, and let us return to the LORD.
Lamentations 3:40

5 Admitted to God, to ourselves, and to another human being the exact nature of our wrongs.

Therefore confess your sins to each other and pray for each other so that you may be healed.
James 5:16

6 Were entirely ready to have God remove all these defects of character.

Create in me a pure heart, O God, and renew a steadfast spirit within me.
Psalm 51:10

7 Humbly asked Him to remove our shortcomings.

Humble yourselves before the Lord, and he will lift you up.
James 4:10

8 Made a list of all persons we had harmed and became willing to make amends to them all.

Do to others as you would have them do to you.
Luke 6:31

9 Made direct amends to such people wherever possible, except when to do so would injure them or others.

Therefore, if you are offering your gift at the altar and there remember that your brother has something against you, leave your gift there in front of the altar. First go and be reconciled to your brother; then come and offer your gift.
Matthew 5:23-24

10 Continued to take personal inventory and, when we were wrong, promptly admitted it.

So, if you think you are standing firm, be careful that you don't fall!
1 Corinthians 10:12

► KEEPING THE PEACE

11 Sought through prayer and meditation to improve our conscious contact with God as we understood Him, praying only for knowledge of His will for us and the power to carry that out.

Teach me to do your will, for you are my God; may your good Spirit lead me on level ground.
Psalm 143:10

12 Having had a spiritual awakening as the result of these steps, we tried to carry this message to others, and to practice these principles in all our affairs.

In the same way, let your light shine before men, that they may see your good deeds and praise your Father in heaven.
Matthew 5:16

This version of the Twelve Steps differs from that used by Alcoholics Anonymous in two places. In Step One the word "alcohol" has been replaced by an underscore. In Step Twelve the word "alcoholics" has been replaced with the word "others". An unmodified version of the Steps is on page 129.

Finding a Twelve Step Group

Most Christian Twelve Step groups are not affiliated with a larger network but are grass-roots ministries in local churches. So the best way to start looking for a group is to phone as many local churches as you can in your area until you find someone who knows about such groups. Some groups choose to identify themselves with larger coalitions of groups–such as those listed below. We urge you to contact these organizations individually for more information about their ministry and approach to recovery. All of them will be happy to refer you to groups in your area if they know of any.

Alcoholics for Christ
1316 N. Campbell Rd. , Royal Oak, MI 48067 .... (800) 441-7877
http://www.alcohholicsforchrist.com

Alcoholics Victorious (A ministry of IUGM)
1045 Swift Street N., Kansas City, MO 64116-4127 .... (816) 471-8020
http://www.iugm.org/av/

Celebrate Recovery
25422 Trabuco Rd. #105-151, Lake Forest, CA 92630-2797 ..... (949) 581-0548
http://www.celebraterecovery.com

N.E.T. Ministries
4235 Mt. Sterling Ave., Titusville, FL 32780 .... (407) 264-2922

New England Assoc. of Evangelicals - Recovery Ministries
279 Cambridge St, Burlington, MA 01803 .... (617) 229-1990

Overcomers Outreach
520 N Brookhurst #121, Anaheim, CA 92801 .... (800) 310-3001
http://www.overcomersoutreach.org

We encourage you not to dismiss the possibility of finding a secular support group that will be helpful to you. Most Christians in recovery today began their recovery journey in a secular support group –and most still find that participation in secular support groups is essential to maintaining their recovery! Look in your local phone book for the phone numbers for A.A. and other resources. Local offices of such organizations as the National Council on Alcoholism and Drug Abuse can also be helpful. Finally, your Country Department of Mental Health can usually help you find local resources. Keep looking until you find what you need!

SOURCES

The Big Book of Alcoholics Anonymous (New York: Alcoholics Anonymous World Services, 1984).

Davis, Martin M., *The Gospel and the Twelve Steps* (San Diego, CA: RPI Publishing, 1993).

Merton, Thomas, *Contemplative Prayer* (New York: Doubleday, 1990).

Miller, J. Keith, *A Hunger for Healing* (New York: HarperCollins, 1991).

Shoemaker, Samuel, *National Awakening* (New York: Harper & Row, 1936).

The Twelve Steps for Christians (Julian, CA: RPI Publishing, 1994).

Twelve Steps and Twelve Traditions (New York: Alcoholics Anonymous World Services, 1983).

The Twelve Steps of Alcoholics Anonymous:
1) We admitted we were powerless over alcohol—that our lives had become unmanageable.
2) Came to believe that a power greater than ourselves could restore us to sanity
3) Made a decision to turn our will and our lives over to the care of God *as we understood Him.*
4) Made a searching and fearless moral inventory of ourselves.
5) Admitted to God, to ourselves, and to another human being the exact nature of our wrongs.
6) Were entirely ready to have God remove all these defects of character.
7) Humbly asked Him to remove our shortcomings.
8) Made a list of all persons we had harmed and became willing to make amends to them all.
9) Made direct amends to such people wherever possible, except when to do so would injure them or others.
10) Continued to take personal inventory and, when we were wrong, promptly admitted it.
11) Sought through prayer and meditation to improve our conscious contact with God, *as we understood Him,* praying only for knowledge of His will for us and the power to carry that out.
12) Having had a spiritual awakening as the result of these steps, we tried to carry this message to alcoholics and to practice these principles in all our affairs.

| RPI Publishing, Inc. | The Twelve Step People |

Now that you've completed *The Twelve Steps: A Spiritual Kindergarten*, we encourage you to look at other recovery resources available from RPI Publishing.

For a complete catalog:
PO Box 44, Curtis, WA 98538
Voice: 800-873-8384
Fax: 360-245-3757
or visit us on-line at:
http://rpipublishing.com/

"Carrying the message to others"

You are invited to become a member of

THE NATIONAL ASSOCIATION FOR CHRISTIAN RECOVERY

P.O. Box 215, Brea, CA 92822
Voice: 714-529-6227
Fax: 714-529-1120
Email: nacr@christianrecovery.com

Visit us on the web at:
http://www.christianrecovery.com/nacr.htm

For Spanish language Christian Twelve Step resources visit:

VENCEDORES

Si tienes problemas de adicción, codependencia o simplemente no estás satisfecho con alguna área de tu vida, has llegado a un buen lugar. Vencedores es una hermandad de personas en recuperación de muchos problemas. Practicamos el programa de los Doce Pasos. A través del apoyo mutuo, la oración y la lectura de la Palabra de Dios, encontramos una serenidad plena, a pesar de nuestras circunstancias aparentes. Somos una organización cristiana, pero no tienes que ser cristiano para participar con nosotros. Esperamos que tú pronto seas Vencedor, también.
Que Dios te bendiga.

http://www.christianrecovery.com/vencedores.shtml